BEATRICE OF BOLDERWOOD

The Diary of a New Forest Girl 1899

Edited by
VERONICA WALTON

with an
INTRODUCTION
by Jude James

New Forest Ninth Centenary Trust
New Forest Museum
2004

Published 2004 by the
New Forest Ninth Centenary Trust
(Charity No. 279373)
with sponsorship

New Forest Ninth Centenary Trust
New Forest Museum
Lyndhurst
SO43 7NY

ISBN 0 9526120 3 8

Printed by
Pardy & Son
Ringwood

A Forest Secret

Oh! There is a nook–if ye will not tell–
Deep down in the forest glade;
And nowhere in the land doth dwell,
A sunnier-hearted maid.

For, oh! She's blithe as a bird on the bush,
That carols all day long,
And morning light till dewy night,
Her heart goes out in song.

Windfall and Waterdrift (1894)
Auberon Herbert
(1838-1906)

By tradition the Tame family understand this short poem
to have be written of Beatrice Ellen Tame

CONTENTS

ILLUSTRATIONS

Colour plates

Text Illustrations

(All illustrations, unless indicated otherwise, are the copyright of Veronica Walton.)

ACKNOWLEDGEMENTS

The diary of Beatrice Ellen Tame would never have been published without the scholarly guidance and academic input made by Jude James. Through his persistent and thorough research the shadowy people from an era long past have been brought into clear focus. They have become so much more than a mere collection of named adults seen through the eyes of a young girl. Jude's local knowledge and love of the New Forest and its history, combined with an historian's thirst for accuracy and detail have made this publication into more than a day-by-day account. He has also enabled readers who are descendants of characters in the diary to find out something of their own families' histories, which adds more appeal and interest to the dairy's content than I could ever have hoped for. He has my especial gratitude and appreciation.

My grateful thanks are also due to all of the following:

Mr and Mrs Chatfield for information on Tom Webb Scamell and his family. Maldwin Drummond for researching the Hendy family of Southampton.

The staff at the Hampshire Record Office for access to the various relevant sources.

Peter Harman for his research on the Morris and Kelly families and the Mersey coasters of the 19th century.

Jamaica Press, Hartland, for photocopying and typing.

Peggy James for reading and advising and proof reading the diary text.

Sarah Kendal, BSc., for typing.

Arthur Lloyd for general historical information on the New Forest and notes on the Retford family.

Jill Morris for access to family papers and information on Jack Kemp Morris and the Kelly family.

The Rev. Peter Murphy for access to the Emery Down parish registers.

Richard Reeves for his research on Bolderwood Lodge and general background information on the New Forest.

Peter Roberts for his dedicated research into several of the individuals recorded in the diary, most especially on the later life of May Forbes in Kent.

Bruce Rothnie of the Forestry Commission for the Bolderwood files.

Southampton Local Studies Library.

Mark Tosdevine, BA, AMA, for historical background, computer searches for reference material, typing and IT help.

Richard Walton, BA, DipTP, FMA, for advising on extra material for the book, IT support, typing and general encouragement throughout.

Cecil Whitfield, Secretary of the Lyndhurst Baptist Church, for his loan of the Baptist Church minute book and general background information on the Baptist families at the time of the diary.

Veronica Walton
July 2004

INTRODUCTION

The diary and diarist

That a farmer's seventeen-year old daughter should so artlessly open a window on late Victorian rural life which is at once enchanting and informative is quite remarkable. It is also something for which we should be grateful. Her revealing diary was written during the year 1899 and seems to have had neither precursors nor successors; so it stands as a unique and rewarding document of Forest life.

Beatrice Tame, the diarist, living with her closely-knit family in an isolated farmhouse called Bolderwood Farm (or Lodge) set deep within the fastnesses of the New Forest, gave her a perspective on life that tells the reader much about the milieu of country life.

Beatrice was born at Bolderwood, in the parish of Minstead, on 15 April 1881. Her father was the first farmer to take the tenancy of Bolderwood Lodge which previous to that time had always been occupied by officers and officials of the Crown. On Lady Day 1879 he entered into a seven-year lease with the Office of Woods for this 26 acre plot with its old farmhouse. With him came his wife Letitia, his elderly father, also Henry, then aged 83, and his eldest son, another Henry, aged four months. The family also included amongst its members two of Henry's orphaned nieces, daughters of his older sister, Elizabeth. They were Annie and Louie Barfoot, then aged respectively, 15 and 14. During the next few years two further sons were born, William in 1883 and Richard in 1887. It is this family group which makes up the key players in the drama of incidents and events so colourfully filling the pages of the diary.

The editor of this remarkable work is Veronica Walton, a granddaughter of the diarist. From the record Beatrice has left us she has distilled the essential elements and then elaborated the many facets to complete a work of considerable range and depth – a work that forever will be valued by all those who are fascinated by life in rural communities and, in particular, the New Forest.

The diary is contained in two red school exercise books (165 mm x 205 mm) each of 60 pages. They have stiff board covers with a sewn binding. Each page is marked with 27 horizontal feint lines, which act as guides for the diarist's pen, and 24 vertical lines. The diary commences on 3 March, 1899 in the first book and concludes with entries for 29 and 30 June written on the back inside cover. It fills every page with the exception of a space of six and half lines left blank for the entry on 16 May.

The Tame Family outside their Bolderwood home 1899
L. to R. Standing: Henry Tame (father), Beatrice (Bee), Richard (Dick), William (Will) and Henry (Harry)
Seated: Letitia Tame (mother) and Henry Tame (grandfather)

The second exercise book opens with the entry for 1 July and concludes on page 25: the remaining 35 pages are wholly blank.

The main group of entries cover 27 weeks of the year 1899, running from the 3 March to the 9 September followed by a final isolated entry for 24 November.

Most of the diary is written in ink with just a few entries in pencil (these changes are noted in the text). The handwriting is relatively decipherable but a few words defy clear identification. The bulk of the entries are made by Beatrice Tame, the diarist, but a few have been inserted either by her brother Henry or a cousin, Sydney Kelly, and there is a single, rather enigmatic, verse written by another cousin, Arthur Webb. These are indicated in the main text.

In general the calligraphy, punctuation and spelling indicate that the diarist had a reasonable elementary education and a grasp of grammar. However, there are some anomalies, most probably a result of writing the diary whilst she was tired or otherwise distracted. Some of the words she uses have now passed from general use, notably 'gathering' describing a swelling, boil or abscess and 'bossed' meaning to make a mistake, to make a mess of or to miss. Abbreviations are fairly well distributed throughout the diary. For example, Lyndhurst is invariably spelled Lyndhst and there are two or three alternative abbreviations for Southampton. Frequently station is abbreviated to St. Often days are shortened as in Wednes. or Satur. Both first names and surnames are often indicated by the initial letter alone. Where there is doubt or for purposes of clarity these have been expanded without comment.

Editorial method.

So far as it is possible the text of the diary has been transcribed as accurately as possible. However, some punctuation has been amended or corrected, *e.g.* words like couldn't and doesn't appear in the diary as could'nt and does'nt. Most contractions have been expanded, especially those of proper names. Minor misspellings where it is judged these are just a slip have been corrected without comment. Others have been retained and the word *sic* added immediately after the word in brackets, thus [*sic*]. This technique has been adopted as it provides an indication about the diarist's spelling ability or, here and there, her general knowledge and more truthfully represents her style.

All other additions, expansions and explanations made by the editor have been set within square brackets but these have been kept to a minimum and are used solely to clarify or improve the reader's understanding of the text.

On two occasions the diarist has added a question mark within round brackets, thus (?), to indicate that she is unsure of the word used. For example, though she correctly uses the dialect word 'pook' (22 June), she feels sufficiently unsure of herself so inserts a question mark after it. These are retained in the transcription.

The diarist occasionally puts words or short expressions in inverted commas. She appears to do this when making an ironical or humorous comment. For example, she uses the description "drorin-room" (9 May) which would seem to reflect an observation on what might be called 'refined usage', especially as it is in the context of decorating rooms ahead of Miss May Forbes's visit. It is not so easy to explain why she wrote 'Morrrrnee' (1 May) for a pony's name, with its surfeit of 'r's, except that it may have been making fun of a pronunciation known to Tame family members.

Beatrice's voice, through her diary entries, tells the story as it occurred. Even the few lapses or lacunae highlight the tiredness she sometimes felt after a strenuous day of work or play and these help to bring the text to life and allow us to get closer to her personality.

The only previous published accounts of the Tame family are the short records penned by Sarah Robinson and recorded in her personal narrative published in 1914, and the better known and fuller description provided by Heywood Sumner in his *Book of Gorley* (1910). In this he describes, perhaps a little too colourfully, the character of 'Old Tame'. In 1987 this became available to a much wider audience with the publication of a facsimile of the original manuscript version of the *Book of Gorley* in a delightful coloured publication entitled, *Cuckoo Hill: The Book of Gorley*, edited by Margot Coatts. This latter version was somewhat fuller and is accompanied by a colour portrait of old Henry Tame, aged 101 and a delightful sketch of Bolderwood Lodge before the extensions were added in 1890. What is interesting is the high regard Sumner evidently had for Henry Tame (Beatrice's father) for he speaks of him, 'as a valued and constant friend'. Heywood Sumner and his bride, Agnes, spent their honeymoon with the Tames at Bolderwood in 1883.

Bolderwood Lodge

The name Bolderwood is also spelt Boldrewood which, in fact, is always used by Beatrice Tame in her diary. Both spellings seem to have been current in the nineteenth century but today Bolderwood has become the accepted, indeed orthodox, spelling as revealed on Ordnance Survey maps, by the Forestry Commission and the Post Office.

Bolderwood Lodge is also called Bolderwood Farm which, strictly, is more correct as it was once the home farm for the now demolished mansion of Bolderwood Lodge. Nearby there is also Bolderwood Cottage, occupied in the time of the diary by the Lane family, employees of the Office of Woods. Some early postcards (around 1905) illustrate Bolderwood Cottage and call it Bolderwood Lodge. I cannot solve the confusion merely record it!

The farmhouse was built of brick with a hipped tiled roof. Two chimney stacks rose from the hips at either end. As is characteristic of such buildings in Hampshire it was symmetrically planned. It would appear to have had eight main rooms, four on each floor, in addition to the usual offices. As can been seen from the Ordnance plan there were small extensions on either side. The front door, with a projecting porch, was centrally placed and this would have opened to a through passage leading to a back door which gave access to the farm yard. The front faced due south. In 1890 a large extension was constructed on the west side and, in 1910, this was further extended. Eight farm buildings can be identified on the OS plan. The farm area was a little less than 27 acres, including an area of rough pasture called The Rails which occupied 10½ acres (now the Deer Sanctuary). By agricultural standards this is a small holding but it also had the right of pasture on the New Forest, which wholly surrounded the farm, and was of great value. Additionally, the right of turbary was granted to Henry Tame at the time he became tenant of the Crown on 25 March 1879. Near the house was an orchard supplying apples for cider which was made on the farm.

Henry Tame had previously farmed at Hill Farm, Thorney Hill in the parish of Bransgore but coming to Bolderwood gave him more opportunity to exploit the resources of his small farm. When Tame's lease came up for its first renewal in 1886 the Deputy Surveyor was to remark in a letter to the Commissioner of Woods, 'I do not think it will be easy to find a better tenant for such a holding'.

On first occupying the farm Henry Tame had to engage casual and seasonal labour to help and had, additionally, the regular assistance of Annie and Louie Barfoot, his nieces. As Beatrice and his older sons Henry and William, grew up so they provided the essential labour on the farm which must have eased the financial situation for the family. It is interesting to note from the diary that Harry (Henry) is to 'pay for his keep' as from 4 March 1899, which was several months before his 21st birthday. It is an indication of how the finances had to be carefully husbanded to make ends meet.

A significant change to the fortunes of the Tame family came when Bolderwood was discovered by the wealthy railway businessman, James Staats Forbes, in about 1888 or '89. How he came upon such a remote location is not known but several clues might help explain

The cider press in operation in the Browse Pen at Bolderwood.
L. to R: Henry Tame, Tobe Gailor, David Broomfield and 'Chummie'

this. Although such evidence is only circumstantial it does help make sense of the events that followed.

Forbes, in addition to all his business enterprises, was a connoisseur of art and certainly known to such prominent artists as Hubert Herkomer (later Sir Hubert von Herkomer) who in due time was to paint a portrait of the businessman. A nephew of Forbes was none other than Stanhope Forbes, the talented and renowned artist who, in the year of the diary was to establish his school of art at Newlyn, Cornwall. Herkomer knew Stanhope Forbes but he also knew Frederick Golden Short of Lyndhurst, who had exhibited at the Royal Academy in the 1890s. Short was on friendly terms with the Tames as is clearly revealed in the diary and, significantly, both Short and the Tames regularly worshipped at the Baptist Church in Lyndhurst. Beatrice tells us in the diary that 'Mr F. Short is gone to Cornwall' (17 June). It would not be at all unreasonable to conclude that his visit was to Stanhope Forbes on the occasion of the establishment of the Newlyn School. We know Herkomer visited the Shorts in Lyndhurst so there was a clear connexion with the three artists and, of course, with James Forbes. It is perhaps not stretching coincidences too far to suggest that Forbes in his quest for a quiet rural retreat should have been told about Bolderwood, known to Frederick Short and, no doubt, to Herkomer also.

Forbes certainly visited Bolderwood in 1889, recorded so wistfully by Beatrice in the dairy when she recalls, 'I have not been in that Inclosure since I was about 8 or 10 years old and went with Mr and Mrs Forbes and Harry...' (21 June). Later Lascelles recalls in a letter to his head office,

> The circumstances however were peculiar, and were these. The late Mr J.S. Forbes, a man of great wealth, who took much delight in coming to stay at Bolderwood Farm in order to obtain entire rest, wanted to improve the accommodation for his own special convenience. He therefore offered to Tame to find the money for the additions he wished for, provided that Tame could, by getting a fresh lease from the Crown, secure him the occupation of them, if and when he chose, for the remainder of his life, which he calculated and rightly so, will be covered by a fresh lease of 21 years. Tame did not spend a penny of his own money at that time. The outlay was nothing at all to Mr Forbes who only wanted security for a term of years; Tame was quite ready to break his lease and start again with a fresh one of 21 years...

Perhaps Lascelles was fully aware of just how peculiar the circumstances were. In 1890 May Forbes, the illegitimate daughter of James Forbes, was 12 years old and there is no reasonable doubt that her doting father wanted a retreat for her and himself. Indeed, it is the start of a long connexion between May and the Tames running on to about 1924.

Bolderwood Farm: the soft fruit garden in the foreground.
The original farmhouse to the right and the large extension to the left

The substantial brick-built extension required by Forbes was added to the west side of the existing farmhouse. It was grander and, architecturally, somewhat incongruous, with its gabled high roof and substantial chimney stacks. It was stated to have cost £376 10s., though Lascelles later states 'upwards' of that cost and later still quotes the sum of £400. By the time of the diary the suite of rooms contained within the extension were May Forbes's lodgings and Beatrice makes references to painting 'all the light paint in the "drorin' room"', which was a room in the extension, in readiness for May's first visit of the year. And on the 5 May she notes, 'Finished getting Miss May's rooms ready. I dusted the whole place pictures and all and I have arranged 28 vases this evening…'.

On another occasion Beatrice is obliged to provide all three meals in the garden for May Forbes and her two guests, Mrs Hughes and her son Sidney from Emery Down, and she complains that it 'made a lot of extra work' (1 August). It is evident that although there was a comfortable, even friendly, relationship between Miss Forbes and Beatrice she was, nevertheless, clearly subservient to her.

By this time Louie Barfoot, Beatrice's cousin, was employed as lady's maid to May Forbes, and travelled with her on her many jaunts.

It is evident that the Tames were able to exploit the extension made to their farmhouse by providing some kind of guest house facility at those times when May Forbes was not in residence. This is rather borne out by the comment on a postcard sent from Alfred Hendy to the Tames stating that he was 'coming on Saturday with Mr and Mrs Mason, if possible, and if the "Hotel" is not full' (9 September). In the 1901 census two boarders and a visitor are recorded as resident. Such use of the house would provide a useful financial supplement to the income realised from the traditional farming activities. Dinners (mainly midday) and teas are also provided from time to time and it speaks highly of the family's enterprise when they were able to rustle up a meal, without prior booking, for Miss Eliott of Bourne School and seven of her girls (15 July). Wednesday, 28 and Thursday, 29 June seemed to be particularly busy days. 'Murray Petty came in to dinner. Two ladies, friends of Mr. Duckworth's, called to see Grandpa and get refreshments, they were cycling. We had lots of visitors yesterday. Miss Eyre and her lady companion to tea and to see Grandpa. Mr and Mrs Jeffreys and two friends to tea and afterwards Lizzie [Hendy] and Mrs and Miss Child and Mrs Pechil.'

The extension to Bolderwood, built in 1890, was formally sublet by Henry Tame to James Forbes for £30 a year. Considering that the rent charged by the Office of Woods for the whole farm was only £38 per annum this clearly shows how valuable the connexion with Forbes was. May Forbes continued this arrangement after her father's death in 1904 and, indeed, arranged for a further substantial extension, designed by Sydney Kelly of Walton, Liverpool, to be built in 1910. This consisted of a kitchen and room downstairs with two bedrooms upstairs, one opening on to an attractive balcony. This work was carried out by H.A. Turner, builder of Lyndhurst, for the sum of £140. In this case, however, a 5% premium was added to the rent of the farm to offset the cost of the building although it had been entirely paid for by May Forbes. The reason for this was that the work carried out improved the farmhouse for the sitting tenant, Henry Tame, and ultimately increased its value to the Crown. It was of no concern to the Office of Woods as to how the project was financed and any subletting arrangements that might exist were entirely at the discretion of the tenant.

Religious life

It is quite evident that the Tame family were deeply committed Christians and Beatrice reveals herself to be quite aware of the bitter controversy over ritualism gripping the Church of England in 1899. It is interesting to recall that Old Henry Tame, Beatrice's grandfather, when attending a service in Bramshaw church, had a revelation recounted so colourfully by Heywood Sumner, 'I was a-looking at the parson and a-thinking – I shan't get much good out o' 'ee – When the Lard call me…his vaice comed out of the wall "This is no place for 'ee" – so I knew I was called for his service, and I comed out of church and never been in one since'. He found in the Wesleyan Methodists a greater empathy and soon became a preacher for them in his own right. By the time the Tame family had moved to Bolderwood in 1879 they had become committed Baptists and Beatrice, in particular, regularly attended the Baptist Church in Lyndhurst. The

Baptist community there consisted very much of local trades people including the Golden Shorts, the watchmaker and jeweller Edward May and Henry Cheeseman, the florist and fruiterer, all of whom figure in the diary. The pastor at this time was the Rev. Tom Webb Scamell who had been trained at Spurgeon College in London. He was evidently an able minister who succeeded in raising the profile of the Baptists in the village and, after the formation of the parish council, became its chairman. He also served as a governor on the board of the Church of England School and on the burial board for the cemetery.

Henry Tame, Beatrice's father, became a trustee of the Baptist Church in 1890. Beatrice herself played the organ there and perhaps had received some instruction in this from Frederick Golden Short who was the regular organist.

When Henry died in December 1914 he was laid to rest in the Baptist Church burial ground and amongst the many mourners were May Forbes and Alfred Hendy. His wife, Letitia, was to follow him in a matter of weeks, dying in January 1915.

One thing that is difficult to explain is why William and Richard Tame were both baptised at Christchurch, Emery Down, by the Rev. Herbert Thomas Hughes and yet Beatrice was not.

May Forbes seems to have mostly attended the church at Emery Down when she was staying at Bolderwood and was on very good terms with the vicar there, the Rev. Herbert Hughes, and his wife, Grace, and only son, Sidney.

Despite this it is apparent that the Tame children did not hold the vicar of Emery Down in high esteem judging by the satirical comments penned by Beatrice's brother, Henry, on 23 May. The elusive initials S.P. following the Chadband name, if decrypted, might provide a fuller insight to Henry's thoughts (see Biographical Notes).

Businessmen and the Tame connexion

One of the more intriguing aspects revealed in the diary is the very close family and personal relationships existing between the rural Tames and various businessmen. Mentioned elsewhere are the close ties with James Staats Forbes, the railway tycoon: but there was also a close relationship with Alderman Richard Kelly, a major and very successful building contractor of Liverpool, and also with the Hendys in Southampton. It is interesting to note that Sydney Kelly, only son of Richard, was visiting the Hendys in Southampton at the time of the 1901 census, which suggests an existing friendly relationship between those families. Perhaps the most curious circumstance arises through the third marriage of 'Old' Henry Tame, then aged 57, to Maria Gell in 1853; how did a gardener in the New Forest meet his spouse? And what a coincidence it seems that one of her daughters, by her first marriage, should have married Richard Kelly, a man firmly rooted in Liverpool. The fact that their daughter, Maria Gell Kelly, should have married in 1894 an enterprising but, in the long run, rather unsuccessful entrepreneur, John Kemp Morris, who aspired to establish a shipping line encourages speculation on the expansion of business endeavour within the wider family. In such a commercial and business milieu is it not likely that James Staats Forbes also had some involvement? Answers to such questions must remain in abeyance until firmer evidence becomes available.

What the diary does not record

Beatrice, in common with so many other similar diarists makes little mention of events beyond the concerns of everyday life. The diary is strictly personal and domestic. Yet major events were occurring in the year of the diary. It may seem odd that she made no mention of the loss of the SS *Stella*, a Southampton vessel, on 30 March 1899, especially as over the following months there were several legal decisions to be made following the recovery of bodies from the disaster which are faithfully reported in the pages of the local newspapers. The fact that the courageous action of the stewardess, Mary Anne Rogers, made her a national heroine should go quite unnoticed speaks either of insularity or a sense of inappropriateness for recording such events in the diary. The lack of a mention of this tragedy seems particularly odd in view of the connexion of the Tames with shipping and the fact that Beatrice's brother William went on holiday with ship-owning cousins in Liverpool on 10 April and returned by sea after a two-day voyage from Liverpool to Padstow (9 May).

Beatrice with her brothers, Harry and Willy in their Burley Troop uniforms

And, although commencing after the main group of entries, the South African (Boer) War broke out in October but earlier in the same year both her older brother Henry and younger brother William enrolled in the New Forest Scouts. This was a uniformed riding troop founded in Burley in 1899, which became K Company of the 4th Battalion of the Hampshire Volunteers; their badge was the 'Rufus Stirrup'. The photograph shows the two boys in their uniforms with Beatrice standing proudly between them with a hand resting on each of their shoulders. This picture must have been taken at the time of the establishment of the troop as the two flashes depicting the Rufus Stirrup do not appear on their collars nor does the one on the upper arm, bearing the device 'Hants 4 V'. It is yet another indication of how closely the Tames were involved in their community. It would have seemed appropriate for Beatrice to have mentioned this activity of her brothers in the diary but she does not do so.

Despite anything that may seem to be lacking the important point is that the publication of Beatrice's diary cannot be seen as anything less than a vehicle provided for increasing our awareness of the many complex and often fascinating interactions of rural folk in the dying year of the 'Naughty Nineties'.

Jude James,
June 2004.

PROLOGUE

Beatrice Ellen Tame was born on 15 April 1881 at Bolderwood Farm in the New Forest. Her father was Henry James Tame who had married Letitia Webb on 8 July 1876. Letitia, the daughter of James and Lucy Webb, was born in 1843 at 11, White Lion Street, Chelsea, London. She was a well educated girl who went to the Diocesan Teacher Training College at Salisbury. At the time of her marriage she was headmistress of a school in Peterborough, thirty three years old, two years older than her husband, who was born in 1845 at Bartley. After their marriage they went to live at Hill Farm, Thorney Hill, Bransgore with Henry's father (also Henry Tame). Nine months later Letitia gave birth to her first child, Florence. Sadly, this baby died when she was only eight months old. In a letter to her niece, Annie, Letitia wrote, on December 21st 1877, '...Now, darling, there are some sad news for you, Jesus has taken our little treasure to be with Him. She died on December 3rd, in convulsions. I know you will be like us, very sorry to lose her, but she is now where we hope one day to be "safe in the arms of Jesus".'

This sad letter gives us an insight into how women coped in those days with frequent infant mortality in childbirth or in the first years of life from illness. The simple belief and the firm faith that they were in God's hands and that after death they would be reunited in heaven with their beloved children if they were taken from them must have been the only way to come to terms with such recurring and frequent tragedies.

Letitia Tame (née Webb), wife of Henry Tame

Diocesan Training College, Salisbury.

A print of the teachers' training college at the time Letitia was a student there

However, a year later in 1878 they had another child, Henry James, who thrived. In 1881 Beatrice Ellen was their first child to be born at Bolderwood into which the family had moved in 1879, followed by her brother William in 1883 and then another brother Richard (Dick) in 1887. The family was then complete and they seem to have enjoyed carefree childhoods, all playing their part in the running of the farm, caring for the cattle and horses and helping with all the seasonal work.

Henry Tame, Beatrice's father, was a reasonably prosperous and successful small tenant farmer. The family employed jobbing workmen and bred a herd of Shorthorn cattle and had a large number of fine ponies. They also kept a few pigs.

As Commoners, they had pasture rights in the New Forest for grazing and also rights of turbary. These rights dated back to Anglo Saxon times, long before William the Conqueror used the Forest for the hunting of deer. Commoners' pasture rights entitled the farmer to turn out a certain number of animals into the forest to graze. They were also allowed to cut turf, gather firewood and dig for the lime rich clay known as marl to serve as fertilizer and improver on the less productive sandy soil. The Tames tilled an area of arable land for their hay and crops. The farm also had a large pasture known as the Browse Pen; now used as the Deer Sanctuary at Bolderwood. The family were fortunate to have benefited from the 1877 New Forest Act often known as 'The Commoners' Charter' which limited the Crown's power to plant timber on grazing land and more fully ensured the commoners' rights.

Letitia educated her family at home and they were all very well-read and excellent at written English. It is obvious from this journal that the four children enjoyed each other's company and were very devoted. It is not surprising that with three lively brothers and a role to play on the farm that Beatrice was a tomboy. She was a brilliant rider and loved horses and the diary reveals a most varied range of activities that she was allowed to do. Her parents must have been very forward thinking and enlightened to have encouraged her to be like this and it is quite surprising that a young Victorian girl should have had so much freedom to do these things, as well as having all the expected virtues of those days for a young lady - singing, playing the piano and organ, studying botany, drawing and painting. She certainly did everything that her brothers did and more. One wonders how she managed it with the restrictions of her clothing, the boned corsets, the flowing skirts and elegant blouses!

Beatrice's diary paints a vivid picture of life, work and play at Bolderwood farm during the spring and summer of 1899, and in it are chronicled a colourful pageant of people parading through its pages! The Tames at Bolderwood were hospitable so that added to their huge circle of friends and relations; there are numerous passing travellers who call. Of course, feeding and accommodating these many visitors also supplemented their income from farming enterprise. Sometimes they called to see the famous old man of the family, their grandfather, who lived with them; sometimes they were just lost walkers in need of directions, always receiving sustenance as well as being put on the right path again. There always seems to have been a bed and a good meal organised in minutes to accommodate all and sundry!

The Life and Times of the Tames of Bolderwood

Much is revealed about the daily life of this typical farming family at the end of the 19th century and in the closing years of Queen Victoria's long reign in Beatrice's diary. The reader also gains a good insight into the

Beatrice poses with bowl and rolling pin on baking day

affairs and activities of Bee's family in particular. This was a time of social change, as well as a time of advancing mechanisation and new scientific discoveries and inventions, and the diary reveals what it was like to be living through this time. In her narrative Beatrice has given us so much more than just a daily account of her life, but we do learn a great deal about her interests and accomplishments. She was an artistic girl, musical, a good singer and competent organist. She had been taught to play the piano by their lodger Miss May Forbes, who was an accomplished musician. Beatrice evidently reached a high standard of piano playing, as she speaks of receiving by post Grieg's latest composition, the *Lyric Pieces*, and said "I'm longing for a practice at them." Her love of flowers and botany laid the foundation for her great skill at flower painting in later life as can be seen in the colour plates of her work reproduced here.

Like many artistic people, Beatrice could be passionate and temperamental. Her mother, Letitia, who was always so dignified and controlled, must have often reproached her for her failings. However, in her diary she shows mostly good humour, compassion for others and unwaning enthusiasm for everything she does.

Beatrice did so much it makes the reader feel quite breathless, how did she fit so much in any one day and still find time to write up her diary by candlelight? She would have been expected to play her part in all the domestic duties of the household; although there was usually a maid in residence as well as her older cousins Annie and Louise. 'Bee' writes of baking, churning, cleaning, decorating, flower arranging and sewing, which were just a few of a whole variety of chores in a late 19th century household. A big house with so many visitors, a grand 'lodger' and a large family, plus farm workers, gave a tremendous workload to all the women of the house.

Preparing food was difficult, yet catering was on a grand scale at Bolderwood Farm. There would have been a coal fired range in the main kitchen, most probably a Bodley. There was also a back kitchen which contained an older type of range that was little more than an iron box in a dog grate. This was needed as a back up and would have efficiently roasted meat and also accommodated saucepans on the hob above. These coal ranges were difficult to control and maintain the right temperature, often resulting in "hard baked tarts" (12 April) and failed meringues.

The saucepans used on the hot plates were of cast iron with enamelled linings and very heavy. With no proprietary scouring materials or detergents, cleaning must have been an arduous task. Pans had to be washed inside and out with water and soda crystals and then scoured with a mixture of salt and fine sand. What a chore it must have been.

Beatrice also writes about making cream. She does not say if the Tames owned an up-to-date mechanical separator, but there was a hint of envy in her diary account of a visit with her mother to see Mr William Davis's farm

The back range at Bolderwood

Beatrice, a very capable horsewoman, sits side saddle
on one of the Tame ponies

and of seeing his new separator at work. This may well have been a New Lister Separator, as patented in 1892. At home their cream was probably made by the slower method of pouring milk into a wide, shallow 'settling' dish made of tin, glazed earthenware or porcelain. After 24 hours, the cream would have risen to the surface and then skimmed off with a wooden saucer like utensil, with very small holes to drain out the finer liquid. Most of this cream would have been put aside to make butter and, at least twice a week, Beatrice, or one of the other female members of the household, would have to do the churning, which was a strenuous and lengthy process.

At Bolderwood they would have had either a box churn, or a simple earthenware plunge churn. As butter and cream consumption must have been very high, I would hope that Bee had a more efficient type of churn than the earthenware one, *i.e.* a box or barrel churn for more 'mass' production. After making the butter the churn had to be thoroughly scalded and cleaned because any dirt, or sour cream residue, would have spoiled the butter produced at the next churning.

When she could escape from the household chores, Beatrice loved to be outside. Sometimes she would just 'mouch' about, as she puts it, with a gun, taking pot shots at the birds in the cherry trees (as encouraged to do by her father), or at rabbits that strayed into the corn. At other times she would go into the Forest to pick wild flowers and blossoms, or simply walk with her friends through the inclosures. She also loved to ride, sometimes bareback, sometimes side-saddle, to fetch the cows from the forest in the evening for milking. This was one of her greatest pleasures and she expressed disappointment in the diary when her brothers got there first.

Another great pleasure was cycling and bicycle maintenance; not surprising as she was such a lively, 'modern' young woman. This was the newest craze in the late 19th century, with 600,000 cycles in use in Britain by 1899. The New Forest was ideal terrain for this mode of transport. Cycling brought a new freedom to all, especially young women. The earlier bicycles were not really suited for girls to ride; however, in order to overcome this deficiency manufacturers soon adapted their designs. The cross bar was lowered and a dress guard and cover put over the chain and back wheel. The 26-inch wheels of Beatrice's bike were smaller and lighter than Mr Barnard's 'old' Singer that she rode round the garden at Bolderwood on 17 April. She said 'it is a Singer but it was not manufactured 4 years ago or 8. The pattern is slightly older than the Model de Luxe... So! I had a ride round the garden on it...and it's a good old "crocklette."'

Her own bicycle, new at the start of this diary, was the latest model, complete with 3 gears, a 26-inch frame and pneumatic tyres. In fact, it does not differ much from a modern lady's bicycle. Beatrice mentions bicycles again and again in her diary and seems to have been the local enthusiast and expert on cycling matters; helping her friends with the mechanics and teaching anyone she can persuade to ride her bicycle - even the grand, distinguished, elderly Mr Forbes (22 May). Beatrice is also delighted to be given 'additions' for her bike, including a modern steel lamp and most exciting of all, a Veeder Cyclometer. There must have been much laughter and teasing when Fred Clark and his friends fitted her cyclometer on the wrong way so that it went into reverse (22 May).

The Tame family was very friendly with the Hendy family from Southampton, whose sons were establishing themselves in the new and growing motor trade. This meant that the Tame children were able to experience the 'joys of motoring'. The Hendy boys seem to have been trailblazers in the latest forms of transport in the Southampton and New Forest areas. On 5 July, Alf Hendy visits Bolderwood on his motor tricycle. This would have been a De Dion Bouton. The 'motelle' referred to by Bee on 20 May was probably a two-seater version. Alf and Lizzie turn up at Bolderwood in the afternoon and she writes; "We heard the bunk, bunk, bunk from afar." On 22 April, when Beatrice went to stay with the Hendys in Southampton, she almost had a go on a 'sociable' tricycle and was probably most disappointed when the jaunt was called off.

Bee often writes with great concern about the suffering of others; including the untimely deaths of friends and acquaintances from illnesses such as influenza, bronchitis, or congestion of the lungs.

Fresh air, plenty of exercise and a good diet ensured that Beatrice and her brothers had grown up healthy and strong. At the time of the diary, the only health problems in the family were relatively minor. There were a few small accidents, such as cuts from farm implements, fainting fits, some short bouts of 'unwellness' and plenty of toothaches!

By 1899, there had been significant advances in health care, including vaccinations against small pox, the founding of sanatoriums to treat tuberculosis and an infirmary in

Annie Barfoot, Beatrice's cousin, and an important member of the Tame household

Lyndhurst. Dental treatment for the Tames meant a trip to Southampton if a tooth needed extraction, although home-spun remedies and days of misery were the norm.

A combination of a cold March wind and an abscess in the tooth caused Bee three days of discomfort, repeated again in May. The standard treatment for a 'gathering' as she called it, was the application of a 'ginger plaster' and to sit by a warm fire. Her cousin, Annie Barfoot, had the misfortune of a painful 'tooth gathering' on her birthday in May. Annie's teeth were in a sorry state so she had to go to the dentist in Southampton on 17 July to have a tooth out. She also needed a "new set of false teeth at the bottom."

It is not surprising that teeth suffered so, as the advent of toothpaste was not until the turn of the century. At Bolderwood they would have prepared their own recipes with ingredients such as chalk, salt, saponis, oil of eucalyptus, borax, powdered oris root, bicarbonate of soda and attar of roses. Toothbrushes were available and brushing encouraged but little could be done once decay had set in.

By the second half of the 19th century, anaesthetics were becoming common and Annie's dentist probably used nitrous oxide gas when extracting her lower teeth.

The local chemist, J. Golden Short of Lyndhurst would have supplied medicines such as Epsom Salts, iodine, cough linctuses, borax powder and assorted tonics, for all the minor ailments.

Beatrice's younger brother, Will, was rather 'run down' after being unwell in the winter. This caused him to have several styes and boils and take to his bed for a few days in March 1899. The family decided that he needed sea air and a holiday. On 10 April he departed for Liverpool with his cousin Sydney and Uncle Dick (Kelly), who was brother-in-law to Grandfather Tame's third wife, Maria. Richard Kelly's wife Maria (née Gell) was the fourth daughter of Maria Tame, who was first cousin of Letitia Tame and widow of Letitia's brother, John. The two families were very close and the Kellys always came on holiday to the New Forest to stay at Bolderwood. He was a JP and a most successful businessman. His eldest daughter Maria (known in the family as Marie) was married to Jack Morris who owned a coastal shipping business. Through this connexion it was arranged that Will should go on a voyage by coaster to Padstow. The Tames had been persuaded to invest money in the coaster company set up by Jack Morris in 1896. Sadly the outcome of this speculation proved to be financially disastrous and the following account of the fortunes of Jack Morris shows just what a risk they had taken.

The coastal shipping firms in the mid to late 19th century were a booming trade and the wider adoption of steam power brought about a great increase in efficiency of coasters for delivery of bulk supplies around the ports of Britain. These sturdy vessels would take coal from Merseyside to the ports of Ireland and the west coast of Wales, Devon and Cornwall, and return with essential cargoes, such as china clay, granite chippings for roads, sand and gravel. They were easy to load and unload at docksides, with their low, shallow holds while the railway network aided the distribution of these essentials, particularly coal, around the country. Jack Morris, was an entrepreneur who would try almost anything in the coastal shipping business. He originally came from the West Country, probably from Fremington, near Bideford, but had settled in the north west, working first as a shipbroker and then becoming manager of the Trafford Steamship Co. Ltd. His first two ships were the *Trafford* (1896) and the *Latchford* (1897) both named after Manchester locations. The *Latchford* was owned jointly by Jack Morris and a Salford businessman. Jack's aim was to establish his own regular coaster steamer service between the Mersey and the ports of the West Country. His first venture went under the title of the Liverpool and North Devon Steamship Co. Ltd.; then he started a second one called the Liverpool and Cornwall Steamship Company. He was the major shareholder in both companies, but other subscribers were Liverpool businessmen, merchants from Barnstaple and Exeter and, of course, the Tames – Letitia and Henry. Morris was an ambitious businessman and he ordered new ships for the companies' services. The first to be delivered was the *Fremington* (1899) followed by the *Robert Burns*, the *Torrington*, and the *Taunton*. These coasters cost from £6,374 to £6,913 each, so this was a very costly investment. However, neither of Jack Morris's companies prospered and debts mounted. He amalgamated the two companies, but his financial problems continued to grow and in 1904 the company took out debentures with several of its shareholders (including the Tames) to raise £7,500, using its three remaining steamers as security. The accounts had showed only one year when a profit had been made and this was for only £4-10s-10d. Debts became so large that the only thing Morris could do was to sell off the ships but even this desperate strategy could not save the Company and in August 1914 it was placed in receivership. However, in spite of all these setbacks Jack Morris continued in business until his death. Unfortunately for Letitia and Henry Tame this event was almost catastrophic for them because, at the time when Jack Morris had been forming his companies and later when the shareholders were asked to take out debentures, the Tames had persuaded some of their friends to invest in the shipping company. Because of this they felt morally obliged to repay their friends for the losses they had incurred from the investments they had encouraged them to make and then faced bankruptcy themselves.

The sea air for Bee's brother Will came in the form of this voyage down the Mersey, into the Irish Sea, round the coast of Wales, down the north west coast of Devon and Cornwall and ending up in Padstow, Cornwall. He was away for four weeks and the train journey home would have been a pioneering trek for him.

Bee refers to his train journey back to the New Forest. The first part of the journey from Padstow to Wadebridge was on the brand new line that had been opened as recently as April 1899, making him one of the very first passengers. This rail link had been made possible by the building of the iron bridge over Little Petherwick Creek. This bridge was an impressive feat of 19th century engineering and a great boost to trade in the region at this time, linking West Country ports and cities to London. From Wadebridge he travelled by train through Instow, via Camelford and Halwill Junction to meet up with Jack Morris at Fremington Quay who was there to unload coal from his coaster, the *Latchford*. Will stayed the night and the next morning he caught a train to Barnstaple and thence onwards to Exeter. He travelled on from there to Salisbury where he changed for Southampton West. The journey was a great adventure for a 15 year-old boy and he came home looking 'brown and well'. Bee was very envious of her brother and said in her diary 'How I should love to go to Cornwall and North Devon etc.'

The family had very firm Christian beliefs that embraced a good ecumenical mix of Anglican, Baptist and Methodist views. The Sabbath was a day to be enjoyed and not, as one might expect a solemn day with no fun or games allowed. Beatrice's grandfather was a staunch Methodist, her mother Letitia was Church of England and had trained as a teacher at Salisbury, yet they all attended the Baptist Chapel at Lyndhurst. Many of their large circle of friends were drawn from the Baptist congregation. Beatrice involved herself in the local chapel's "good works" by fund-raising, writing out religious journals for Mr Sampson the local Baptist missionary, making dolls, helping out with Sunday School treats and playing the organ for services. The Tame children had been brought up in a household where Christianity was an integral part of life and their unquestioning faith and simple Christian outlook lasted all their lifetimes. Many of the books they enjoyed and read to each other were of a religious nature. Bee herself, without ever actually mentioning God in her diary, had already at the age of eighteen developed very strong views about worship. She speaks of her strong dislike of High Church practice when she wrote her diary on Sunday 23 April after attending the service at St Luke's Church Southampton. She refers to John Kensit, by writing that she wished she had heard him speak when he was in Southampton. Kensit was a Protestant agitator, who at that time was speaking out against the growing tide of ritualism in the Church of England and, with his supporters, organised interruptions to services of which they disapproved. A near neighbour of the Tames, Sir William Harcourt, was also campaigning against 'ritualistic lawlessness' which could well have influenced her views. His series of letters to *The Times* led to the banning of incense in Church of England services by the Archbishops of Canterbury and York in 1899.

Grandfather Tame, the patriarch of the family, without doubt had the strongest influence on his family in religious matters. He had been a Wesleyan preacher for most of his life and was well known locally, partly because of this as well as for his great age. At the time of the diary he was already 103 and still active and healthy with a keen mind and a sociable nature. He enjoyed the attention he received from visitors, having his photo taken, telling people his life story and imparting his fervent religious beliefs to all who talked with him.

One of his frequent visitors was the New Forest author and artist, Heywood Sumner. He had been a major figure in the Arts and Crafts Movement in the 1880s and was a writer and artist of great distinction. Who later became an archaeologist of importance working mainly in the New Forest, Cranborne Chase and south Wiltshire.

In *The Book of Gorley*, published in 1910, Sumner includes a chapter called 'Cottage Chronicles' in which he tells of his visits to Bolderwood in the 1880s and the 1890s and recounts some of his long talks with Old Tame (as he called him). He says how impressed he was by the mental activity of such an aged man and tells us how Old Man Tame, aged over 100, spent time every day writing texts on pieces of paper then carefully wrapping them around smooth stones. These were then given to the keepers' children to place on the road sides leading to Minstead and Lyndhurst for passers by to pick up and read, thus still spreading the word of the Lord.

Heywood Sumner asks the old man how he can read the Bible every day with poor eyesight and asks if B (Beatrice) reads to him, but the answer he gives is that 'the Lord reads to me'. This was because Old Man Tame knew the whole New Testament from memory.

The Old Man also told Heywood the story of his conversion to Methodism and how he 'confounded his enemies' with the power of prayer on many occasions. When Sumner mentioned to Old Man Tame that he has ridden over to Bolderwood on his bicycle, the old man said 'another of the works of the Devil'.

Sumner describes the old man as a 'point of interest in the Forest like one of the most ancient trees', which was a most apt comparison to make.

Old Henry Tame lived in the last few years of the 18th century, through the entire 19th century and into the 20th century. He was born in 1796 at Isleworth in Middlesex. When Henry Tame died his biography was recorded in his obituaries in many newspapers.

These obituaries, written at the time of his death, paint a vivid portrait of Grandfather Tame and it is not surprising that he attracted much attention towards the end of his life. His family were devoted to him and in spite of his stern religious belief; he was a kindly, gentle and tolerant patriarch to his family.

Veronica Walton
August 2004

THE RECENT DEATH OF A CENTENARIAN. — As announced last week, the death of Mr. Henry Tame, of Boldrewood Lodge, took place on Thursday, the 1st inst., at the age 103 years. It may be interesting to our readers to know a little of the well-known centenarian's life. The deceased was born on March 2nd, 1796, at Isleworth, Middlesex, which place he left when a child, his parents removing with their family into Berkshire. The deceased was early employed as keeper of sheep, and at the age of twelve could pitch his fold to the admiration of his seniors. We next find him employed in the gardens of the Duke of Devonshire at Chiswick, and it was interesting to hear him speak of the picturesque costumes worn by the noblemen of the day with their swords always at their sides. When some twenty years of age he journeyed his way to Southampton and was engaged in the nurseries of Mr. Page. While there one of the tasks allotted to him was assisting in the laying out of the Rectory grounds of Whippingham, I.W. We then trace him to the Warrens, Bramshaw, and find him eighty years ago gardener to Mr. George Eyre, grandfather of the present Mr. Briscoe Eyre. He subsequently occupied similar positions in the neighbourhood, never again, we believe going far away from the Forest. At the age of eighty-four he came to reside with his son at Boldrewood, and as the farm belongs to the Sovereign of the Realm, the old man was ever pleased to think of his son as a tenant of the Queen. At this age he did not cease to be active; indeed, up to the age of ninety-five he managed his son's garden for several seasons, doing the whole of the work himself. In fact, since the attainment of his 100th birthday he has interested himself with the flower borders round the house of his Forest home. Many other interesting things could be written of this New Forest centenarian's useful and honourable life; but we will only add that he gently breathed his last on the night of Thursday, February 1st, just before twelve o'clock. His remains were laid to rest in the burial ground of the Lyndhurst Baptist Chapel on Wednesday. The chief mourners were Mr. Henry Tame (his son), Henry, William and Richard Tame (grandsons), Mr. Croxford (son-in-law), Messrs. Richard Kelly and Son from Liverpool, and many others. The service was conducted by the Pastor (the Rev. T. Webb Scamel). The coffin was of elm, with brass fittings, and breastplate bearing the inscription—"Henry Tame; died Feb. 1st, aged 103." The funeral arrangements were carried out by Mr. Gale of Lyndhurst, in a most satisfactory manner.

SOUTHAMPTON TIMES AND HAMPSHIRE
EXPRESS
FEBRUARY 10, 1900

A MAN WHO LIVED IN THREE CENTURIES

To have lived in the seventeen, eighteen and nineteen hundreds was the unique experience of the late Mr. Henry Tame, who recently died at Boldrewood, his New Forest home.

Soon after his birth at Isleworth on March 2nd, 1796, the deceased was moved with his family into Berkshire, and was early employed as a keeper of sheep, after which he was gardener at the Duke of Devonshire's park, Chiswick, and he often recounted how the noblemen of that time wore picturesque costumes, with swords at their sides.

In 1816 Mr. Tame found employment at a nursery in Southampton, and of the landscape gardening he was en-

THE LATE MR. TAME WHO LIVED IN THREE
CENTURIES

gaged in laying out may be noted the pretty rectory grounds at Whippingham, a favourite spot of the late Prince Consort. Eighty years ago the deceased was gardener on an estate bordering the New Forest, finally settling down on his son's farm at Boldrewood on attaining eighty-four, continuing to actively work for another eleven years, and even after his hundredth birthday interested himself with the flower-beds bordering his forest home.

His exact age at death was one hundred and three years and eleven months, yet he was comparatively hale to the last. Not long before he died he ordered a new pair of boots and desired them to be made strong.

On being asked when he first felt age creeping upon him, Tame replied that it was between seventy and eighty, on carrying out some hedging and ditching, that he felt his back ache.

Boldrewood is one of the most delightful parts of the New Forest, and is remarkable for the considerable number of sub-tropical trees that were so successfully planted there many years ago.

Mr. Tame was a sturdy Nonconformist, and is buried in Lyndhurst Baptist Chapel graveyard.

THE GOLDEN PENNY
March 24, 1900   235

A WONDERFUL OLD MAN

'THE PATRIARCH OF THE NEW FOREST.'

A QUAINT and interesting character has just passed away in the New Forest—a wonderful old man who was born before the Battle of Trafalgar, and had almost completed his hundred and fourth year when he died. Visitors to Lyndhurst and the neighbouring parts of the Forest may have picked up here and there stones wrapped in pieces of paper on which texts of Scripture had been written. These were prepared by the centenarian 'Patriarch of the Forest,' written out legibly in his own hand, in hope that they might prove a word in season to the finders. He used to say, 'It's all I can do now.' Boldrewood Farm, not far from Mark Ash, where the oaks and beeches are finest, was the home of Henry Tame. He lived there with his sons and grandsons on Crown property, the Queen's oldest tenant. Not much education was to be had in his young days, but he had learnt to read and write before he became a ploughboy. Later on he took to shepherd's work, and to the last showed a special fondness for the pastoral similes and characters in the Bible. From shepherding he passed to gardening, in which he made himself so proficient as to take very good posts. He was a great walker, and on one occasion covered the distance between Farnham and Christchurch in one day—about seventy miles. At the age of eighty-five he still used to walk four miles to church. In early life Henry Tame was a Wesleyan, and his honest, sterling nobility of character spoke well for the Methodism of those first days. He had a remarkable knowledge of the Bible, having the greater part of the New Testament by heart. His modest and unassuming demeanour and courteous manners won respect and goodwill, and his quaint and original criticism of men and things showed much shrewdness and sagacity. Characteristic traits were his abhorrence of waste and cruelty. With vivid recollections of the time when *white* bread was unknown among the poor, he could not bear to see even a crust thrown away, and the children of the New Forest would have incurred much rather than face his reproof for torturing bird or beast. As his age became extreme most of his time was spent in his chair, which was still older than himself. Yet until his last illness he was always able to shave himself. Influenza brought the illness which proved fatal. Only a few days before the last he repeated the whole of the twenty-third Psalm, and recalled an incident of his boyish shepherding of which the Psalm reminded him. At this time he asked one of his grandchildren, 'How old am I?' On being told he took a sheet of paper and wrote in clear letter, 'Ceased to work at 103.' Then he quietly took to his bed, from which he never rose again.

In the pretty churchyard of the little Baptist chapel at Lyndhurst there was buried a notable man, Mr. Henry Tame, who was known as the centenarian of the New Forest. He was born at Isleworth in 1796, and died at the ripe age of 103. To the last he retained possession of all his faculties, and only took to his bed two days before his death. While serving his apprenticeship as a gardener at the Duke of Devonshire's house at Chiswick, he secretly married his first wife in the year of the great Frost Fair on the Thames—1814. With many a chuckle he used to tell how his only chance of seeing his spouse was to steal out of bed after his fellow-apprentices were sound asleep, drop out of the window, and return to the place again in the early hours of the morning. Latterly much of his spare time was spent in writing his ideas and thoughts on passages of the Bible. The day before he died he asked his granddaughter how old he was, and, taking the book in his hands as with some prophetic insight, the fine old man legibly wrote: "Ceased to work at 103," and lay down on the bed from which he never rose again.

THE DAILY TELEGRAPH
SATURDAY, FEBRUARY 10, 1900

An identical report in
THE GLOBE
SATURDAY, FEBRUARY 10, 1900

THE CHRISTIAN WORLD
MARCH 8, 1900

15

THERE has just passed away in the neighbourhood of the New Forest one who deserves a place in these columns by reason of the great age to which he attained. Had he lived but a few days more Henry Tame would

A Centenarian.

have reached the extraordinary age of 104, for he was born in March, 1796. Until he reached the age of 84 this remarkable old man was actively employed as a gardener, and loved to talk of the picturesque

PHOTO SHORT, LYNDHURST

costumes of the gallant noblemen who strutted about the gardens of the Duke of Devonshire at Chiswick, where he was once employed. The latter years of his life he spent at Boldrewood with his son, and it was his great pride to think of his son as a tenant of the Queen. Up to the age of 95 he looked after his son's garden for many seasons, doing all the work himself, and even after reaching his 100th birthday he interested himself in the flower borders round his Forest home.

THE KING
March 17th, 1900

The funeral of Mr. Henry Tame, who had reached the ripe old age of 103, took place on Wednesday, the service was held at the Baptist Chapel, and was numerously attended. The principal mourners were his son and three grandsons, Mr. Croxford (son-in-law) and Mr. Richard Kelly and his son, who came all the way from Liverpool. The coffin was a handsome one of elm, with heavy brass fittings, and on the breast-plate was the inscription:

HENRY TAME
Died February 1st, 1900
Aged 103 years.

The Rev. T. W. Scamell, pastor of the chapel, read the service, and offered up a beautiful prayer. The arrangements were entrusted to Mr. J. E. Gale.

THE HAMPSHIRE ADVERTISER
COUNTY NEWSPAPER
February 10, 1900

Calendar for the year
1899

January
Sun.	1	8	15	22	29
Mon.	2	9	16	23	30
Tue.	3	10	17	24	31
Wed.	4	11	18	25	
Thur.	5	12	19	26	
Fri.	6	13	20	27	
Sat.	7	14	21	28	

February
Sun.		5	12	19	26
Mon.		6	13	20	27
Tue.		7	14	21	28
Wed.	1	8	15	22	
Thur.	2	9	16	23	
Fri.	3	10	17	24	
Sat.	4	11	18	25	

March
Sun.		5	12	19	26
Mon.		6	13	20	27
Tue.		7	14	21	28
Wed.	1	8	15	22	29
Thur.	2	9	16	23	30
Fri.	3	10	17	24	31
Sat.	4	11	18	25	

April
Sun.		2	9	16	23 30
Mon.		3	10	17	24
Tue.		4	11	18	25
Wed.		5	12	19	26
Thur.		6	13	20	27
Fri.		7	14	21	28
Sat.	1	8	15	22	29

May
Sun.		7	14	21	28
Mon.	1	8	15	22	29
Tue.	2	9	16	23	30
Wed.	3	10	17	24	31
Thur.	4	11	18	25	
Fri.	5	12	19	26	
Sat.	6	13	20	27	

June
Sun.		4	11	18	25
Mon.		5	12	19	26
Tue.		6	13	20	27
Wed.		7	14	21	28
Thur.	1	8	15	22	29
Fri.	2	9	16	23	30
Sat.	3	10	17	24	

July
Sun.		2	9	16	23 30
Mon.		3	10	17	24 31
Tue.		4	11	18	25
Wed.		5	12	19	26
Thur.		6	13	20	27
Fri.		7	14	21	28
Sat.	1	8	15	22	29

August
Sun.		6	13	20	27
Mon.		7	14	21	28
Tue.	1	8	15	22	29
Wed.	2	9	16	23	30
Thur.	3	10	17	24	31
Fri.	4	11	18	25	
Sat.	5	12	19	26	

September
Sun.		3	10	17	24
Mon.		4	11	18	25
Tue.		5	12	19	26
Wed.		6	13	20	27
Thur.		7	14	21	28
Fri.	1	8	15	22	29
Sat.	2	9	16	23	30

October
Sun.	1	8	15	22	29
Mon.	2	9	16	23	30
Tue.	3	10	17	24	31
Wed.	4	11	18	25	
Thur.	5	12	19	26	
Fri.	6	13	20	27	
Sat.	7	14	21	28	

November
Sun.		5	12	19	26
Mon.		6	13	20	27
Tue.		7	14	21	28
Wed.	1	8	15	22	29
Thur.	2	9	16	23	30
Fri.	3	10	17	24	
Sat.	4	11	18	25	

December
Sun.		3	10	17	24 31
Mon.		4	11	18	25
Tue.		5	12	19	26
Wed.		6	13	20	27
Thur.		7	14	21	28
Fri.	1	8	15	22	29
Sat.	2	9	16	23	30

Easter Sunday: 2 April

The Diary
The diary of Beatrice Ellen Tame from March 1899 to November 1899

March 3rd Friday. Mother [Letitia Tame] went to Southampton and bought the paper and carpet for the sitting room, etc. Sent some flowers to Mrs. Best, it is her birthday today. Mother saw Mrs. Evans who was in bed with her face still swollen and poor Mrs. Hendy is no better. Mother got Annie [Barfoot] and me 2 such pretty vases for Mrs. E[vans]'s birthday, on the 14th. Mr. Venvell drove up to fetch Mr. Barnard home, he did not stay long. Willie Jeanes rode up with a telegram from Mr. Forbes for Grandpa [Henry Tame, senior] with congratulations. Dressed my black speaking doll to sell for Mr. Sampson's benefit[1].

Mar. 4. The weather seems inclined to change, it has been cloudy and heavy today at times. Grandpa had letters from Miss M. Harris and Mrs. C. Tame to wish him happiness[2] – Mrs. T. wants to come down. Harry [Tame] and Willie [Tame] have gone over to Mrs. Taylor's on the bicycles for the evening. Did some more enameling [sic]. Mr. C. Seymour has sent Mr. Sampson's Journal to us to read and photographs to see of him and his fellow missionary. Mr. Sampson has grown a beard and looks so different now. Mother and I will have to copy it all. Harry is to pay for keep.

Mar. 5. Drove to Chapel[3] and stayed to Communion afterwards. Harry, Will and Dick [Tame] each cycled. Lilly May rode a little way with us and we have asked her to come up next Sunday with us. Mrs. Evans was at chapel for the first time since her illness. Willy had a letter from Maude [Webb] and Grandpa a card, also a letter from Fanny. Mr. & Miss Gibbins walked over from Stoney Cross to see Grandpa and stayed to tea, she seems a nice, jolly girl. Mr. Squires came up too and he stayed to tea. He looked at all the photos Mr. Sampson has taken and read part of his Journal, it is most interesting.

Mar. 6. I rode to Lyndhurst to buy a whitewash brush as we had none and wanted to start on the sitting room today. Had a chat with Mr. & Mrs. Venvell and Hubert. He says he is much better after his stay at the Infirmary and Mr. & Mrs. V. may come up tomorrow. Mixed up the green paint for the sitting room and we have stripped the walls and the boys have washed the ceiling. Wrote to Mr. Forbes for his birthday tomorrow and we commenced copying the Journal. The meal came up.

Mar. 7. Mr. Forbes' birthday[4], sent him some flowers and letters. At last Maude has written. I was getting very impatient, and now don't know why she hasn't written as she says she will write *soon*. Marie [Morris, née Kelly] wrote to say that she and Mr. Morris will be in Southampton on Friday next and would like to come on with Dad [Henry Tame, junior] and stay until Monday. Mr. Venvell and Hubert drove up with the oats, they wouldn't come in and didn't stop long. Harry whitewashed the sitting room ceiling and Mother has begun papering it and Dick and I began painting it and Annie rubbing up the furniture. Varnished and stained 4 of the brackets. Mr. Cheeseman and his boy and Fannie and Alfie came up to do Miss May's plot, or what we lend her. A. & F. are amusing young monkeys, we had them with us all the afternoon and at tea.

Mar. 8. Finished painting the first coat in the sitting room, and Mother finished the papering. After dinner I rode to Lyndhurst to get some paint, got 4lb. Met Mrs. Evans and Miss [Mary Ann] Short and she walked up with me as far as Swan Hill. Got the receipt from Mr. Millard for the harness for Mr. Waterhouse. Had tea with Mrs. Marshall[5] and Frank [her son] and called on Mrs. Bashford and she gave me some lovely violets. It came onto rain whilst I was at Mrs. M's when the first shower came on and just got home before the 2nd. Found some blackthorn out on the Green. Varnish the mantleboard and one bracket and mixed the paint for tomorrow. They threshed again. Rain.

---

[1] The doll is a donation to a charitable collection organised by Mr. Sampson
[2] Grandpa, *i.e.* Henry Tame, senior, is celebrating his 103rd birthday
[3] The Baptist Chapel in Chapel Lane, Lyndhurst
[4] Mr. James Staats Forbes was celebrating his 76th birthday
[5] Mrs. Jane Marshall, the sub-postmistress at Lyndhurst (see biographical notes)

Mar. 9. Fine day. Painted all the light paint in the "drorin-room" and we got the carpet down and things in and all the rest and it looks so nice and clean. We are so glad to have it done. Got a lot of fern and primrose roots for Auntie [-?] and Lizzie [Hendy]. Prepared for tomorrow as I'm going in to fetch out my new machine. Miss May [Forbes] and Louie [Barfoot] both wrote, they had a pleasant journey and are enjoying Florence. Hope I shall like my new machine.

Mar. 10. Went to Southampton to get my new bicycle, it is a very nice one I think, "Sparesbrook National" 26 ins. frame and 3 gears, A B Tyres, plain black enamel. Alf [Hendy] has given me a bag and spanner and oil can. Percy [Hendy] rode out as far as Millbrook on the Motor Tricycle and then the lamp went out, petrol used up, he didn't think of looking at it before starting; he thought he could just get home. Had a nice ride. Wery tyred!! Marie wrote to say that they can't come as Jack's [Morris] vessel had not arrived. Mr. Sims wrote for the specimens of the trees that I gather from. Promised to get some dandelions for Uncle James [Tame].

Mar. 11. Finished painting the sitting room and did some more of the pictures with gold paint. Had a letter from Elsa, both her mother and her brother are ill and she is busy. Miss [Louisa] James, the Minstead School Master's daughter, called this afternoon. She is collecting for a testimonial for Mr. Maturin[6] as he is leaving in three weeks time. Harry and Will and Dick each went out to look for Dick's heifer and Arthur and Fred Gailor brought her home this evening, they found her. Put my rests and carrier on my new bicycle.

Mar. 12. Rode my new bicycle to Chapel and got down to Sunday School in time to play them two hymns. One of Mrs. Payne's girls asked me for something for her card so I gave her a shilling, so did Annie. Amy said she would come up this week. Mother finished reading Mr. Sampson's Diary to us.

Mar. 13. Started at Mother's bedroom and Harry washed the ceiling and we partly stripped the walls. Hubert [Venvell] drove Mr. Barnard up and he has started at the spare bedroom. Washing day. Wrote a long letter to Maude and Alice and got some ivy for Louie. Dada is ploughing the piece in the lower meadow. Mother wrote to Miss May and Annie to Louie.

Mar. 14. I've got a bit absent minded over the month, I think. Sent off Maude's letter and the match box, Will's birthday gift to her; and the ivy and some flowers to Louie and some flowers to Aunty Rye [Maria Kelly]. Started paperhanging and painting in the bedroom and Harry whitewashed the ceiling. Mr. Shaw, the Missionary to the Gypsies[7] called to see Grandpa, stayed to tea, he is a nice old gentleman. Mother and Annie are getting very tired. I stand fire alright! Harry and Will went to Lyndhurst to have the little chestnut mare shod. She has only been in the trap twice, also they are going to Mr. Brown's to see about the colt. Copied more of the Journal. Miss Annie Payne wrote to me to ask me to take up a chain letter but I wrote and told her that I did one once before and it was all a fraud this one is from New S. Wales and so was that. A notice was put in the papers about them, you have to send 16 used stamps and get 3 friends to take up your letters and so on and on and on. Mr. Brown was not at home, they missed him so they returned Stoney Cross way. Will posted my Bank Book for interest.

Ploughing The Piece at Bolderwood

---

[6] Mr. Maturin is the Rev. Charles Maturin, curate at Minstead. (see biographical notes)

[7] Missionary to the gypsies. This was generally an Anglican inspired effort to bring members of the gypsy families into Christian faith and get them to celebrate their marriages in churches. It was a project that continued well after the First World War.

Mar. 15. Finished the light paint in Mother's room and Mother did more papering. Wrote a good bit of the Diary. Mrs. Evans's birthday, she and Mr. E. drove up to tea and I have lent them *Many Cargoes*[8] and several other books and returned Mrs. E.'s. It was so nice to have them. Mrs. E. was so pleased with her vases.

Mar. 16. Painted the dark paint in Mother's room, papering progressing. Had a nice long letter from Eveline [Burrows], she was so pleased with the snowdrops I sent them. They are her mother's favourite flowers. Went out and got some primrose roots and rhododendrons for Mrs. Mason and got some primroses and other "pretties". Annie wrote to Mother and Aunty Ria [Maria Kelly], Uncle Dick [Kelly] and Sydney [Kelly] are coming down at Easter, we are all so very glad.

Mar. 17. We got the carpet down in Mother's room and began getting it straight. Harry went to Southampton and had his tooth out, it is a huge one and it was an awful pull. Mrs. Hendy is better. I am glad and hope she will continue so. Annie's wheel has not come. Dad says Georgie [-?] is coming on Thursday before Good Friday, and I am to meet him at Lyndhurst on my bicycle.

Mar. 18. We finished putting Mother's bedroom straight, it looks so nice and clean. Dada went to see Mr. Young about the calf. Got my Bank book back. Annie received the Manetha[?] bicolour from Mr. and Mrs. H. Stephenson, it was broken rather. Mother had a letter from Mrs. Farrance saying that Mrs. Pearse is dead. She had been ill a fortnight with influenza, we are all so sorry. Mrs. Epps still has rheumatism very badly and Auntie[9] is as well as can be expected. Received Centenary[10] letter to all Gleaners and Annie and I are going to collect 100 farthings as asked and earn a Centenary Card. Herbert [-] gave us a halfpenny and Mother gave me 2^{d}.

Mar. 19. We all drove to Chapel. Took Annie S. some books. Fine cold day. Annie and I went for a walk and got some flowers for Aunt Annie's birthday.

Mar. 20. Very cold day, stiff wind, there was sleet on the ground when we got up and we've had several snow storms today. We are spring cleaning Annie's bedroom, the boys have scraped the walls and washed them down ready for tomorrow. Mother and I cleaned out the dining room cupboard and Mother papered it and I painted it. Had toothache. Made a rooster Easter Egg.

Mar. 21. Aunt Annie's birthday. Annie and I wrote to her and sent her some flowers and Mother wrote to. Sent Mrs. Marshall a few flowers also. Exceedingly cold day, several storms. Had a letter from Elsa, her mother has been seriously ill with bronchitis and congestion of the lung and she has been sitting with her night and day. No letter from Maude or Louie. My face and teeth began aching after tea, so badly and I went off to bed and lit a fire and put on a ginger plaster and enjoyed myself generally. I did not sleep till about 10 though. I was so cold and the aching a bit chronic; a gathering[11] I think.

Mar. 22. My face is swollen but the pain is better. It began aching again in the morning but on the whole is not so bad today. Painted Annie's room and Mother and Annie scrubbed it etc., and put down the oilcloth. More snow storms. Wrote to Murray Petty for Harry, he took Poppet to be shod this morning and they have been at marl[12] cart. Willie fetched the calf from Mr. Young's. Alf is giving a Magic Lantern Entertainment at the Chapel to the children tonight, we have none of us gone, it's so cold and my phisog[13] prevents me. They are marl digging and carting now. Will has got a nasty boil by his left arm and two styes on his eye. We finished correcting Mr. Sampson's Journal and waited up for Alf but he never came. Went to bed at 12.00 p.m.

---

[8] *Many Cargoes* a popular collection of humorous tales by W.W. Jacobs, first published in 1896.

[9] Auntie is Sarah Farrance, wife of Walter Farrance (see biographical notes).

[10] Presumably this is some kind of charitable collection that is to commemorate the close of the century. The 100 farthings represents 2s. 1d.

[11] A gathering is an abscess or boil. The word has passed out of general usage.

[12] Marl is heavy clay, often with small fossil shells. It is used to add body to the thin Forest soils. One of the rights the New Forest commoners had permitted the collection of marl from appropriate and allocated pits.

[13] A colloquialism for face, being the abbreviation of physiognomy.

Mar. 23. [28 written in error] Another bitterly cold day. Several snow storms, one very heavy one but it all disappeared very soon. We stripped the dining room and took the carpet up and Harry washed the ceiling. They killed Mr. Young's calf, it is nice and fat and a good weight. I wrote the Memo for it. Stained and varnished the chest of drawers in Annie's room. Answered Elsa's letter and sent in my Notice of Withdrawal[14].

Mar. 24. Not quite so cold, though bad enough. The boys finished the dining room ceiling and we got the room straight. Also, we stripped mine and they've started on it. One of my kittens died, poor little darling. Mr. Murray Petty came and brought his young mare. Harry has bought her and we think she will make a nice little cob; she is dark brown and three years old. Mr. P. stayed to dinner. Mr. Evemy, Mr. Hutchens and Mr. Georgie Eldridge came colt-lambing[?] and Will rode Mr. E.'s horse and helped them get their mares. Both Harry and Will went with Murray P. and found his mare and got her in. Mrs Hendy is better, we sent her two of the calves' feet, and she was pleased. Trimmed my best hat with brown satin and steel buckle and ornament and two large quills, it's much better now. Feel much better, but we've each got nasty colds.

Mar. 25. Heavy rain this evening and cold. Cleaned up Annie's bicycle, the "over-haul" before selling it. I hope it will prove a good machine to her. Had letters from Miss May and Miss Winder. She returned Mr. Sampson's Circulating letter to me and is interested about him. Got my Demand order. Frank Lane came to tea, he brought down a letter card from Lou, which he had picked up, dropped by the Post boy I expect. Mr. Lambert has written to know if he can come and stay with us a week. Maude wrote to Mama and Willie and sent Uncle's photo, it is very good of him. Auntie Polly wrote to Mother and sent some newspaper cuttings. Painted my room and stained and varnished my cupboard and bracket. The boys rode the new young mare, she went very well considering it's the first time, she is pretty plucky, gay but not gaudy! Will has got an awful boil by his arm, poor lad.

Mar. 26. Will stayed in bed all day, and Harry for the morning. Had a nice long letter from Maude. Grandpa had a present of £1 from Miss A. Eyres [*sic*].

Mar. 27. Put my room straight and we got the carpet down. Washing day too. Packed the photos for Miss May. Harry rode the young Mare to be shod and they put her in trace harness this afternoon, she went capitally. Wrote to Maude.

Mar. 28. No letters. Will has had a book sent to him from Maude. *Robert Bruce* by Sheldon. I sent her my letter and a bunch of violets. Rode to Lyndhurst and got my money from the Post Office. Mrs. Marshall gave me 2 lovely cyclamen, one white, the other bright pink, and some fern. Mr. Cheeseman showed me his glass houses and gave me some violets from his frame, his flowers are very lovely. I saw some freesia for the first time, to know it, it's heavenly. Bought a pair of brown shoes and things for Mother as well. Very windy ride but I enjoyed it very much. Dear little Alfie and Fannie were so funny. I gave them a penny each to get some chocolate, much to their delight! I saw Mrs Venvell and the bicycle she has just bought. Sent off the photos of the rooms to Miss May at her request.

Mar. 29. Baked and Churned because of Dada's going to S'th'pton tomorrow, being Good Friday this week. Grandpa gave us 6d each, Annie and I, to our Centenary Fund. Went out and found some box-leaved berbery[15] [*sic*] in bloom and a few primroses and *arbor vitae*[16].

Mar. 30. Uncle Dick [Kelly] and Sydney [Kelly][17] have come, they met Dada at Lyndhurst Road[18]. It is so nice to have Uncle with us again. Harry put his young mare in the trucks for the first time between the shafts, she pulled well. Mrs. Marshall sent me a paper to sign for my money, so I wrote to her. Sent Willie's wheel in to be repaired in its breadth. The hounds were very close today and there was a very full hunt.

---

[14] For Beatrice to withdraw money from her Post Office account
[15] Barberry, a thorny shrub with yellow flowers and red berries (*Berberis*)
[16] Tree of Life, a conifer related to the cypress
[17] Sydney Kelly became an architect and was engaged by May Forbes to design the further extension to Bolderwood Lodge in 1909: he signs as S.A. Kelly, FSI (plans in TNA: F 10/10)
[18] Lyndhurst Road about 3 miles east of Lyndhurst, is the nearest railway station to Bolderwood (it is now called Ashurst New Forest).

Mrs. Hendy is rather better. Sydney has not grown at all ['lies' interlined above in Sydney's hand]. Had a few very gentle showers.

Mar. 31. Good Friday. Spent a quiet day. The boys have gone to see Mr. Taylor and the colts, Sydney too, and have not got back yet, it has gone 9 o'clock. Annie and I went out for a ride on our bicycles this afternoon, but it was very windy and tired Annie. Uncle Dick and Dickie and I went for a little walk just before dark. Harry paid Mr. T. for the mares for six weeks.

April 1st. Have not been made a fool of! It has been a beautiful fine day for the 1st. Miss A. Eyre sent a parcel of shawls. We all had a tune up this evening together [with] old songs, *Poor Old Joe*[19], etc. They have been planting the piece in the lower meadow with potatoes. Will rode Jessie in to be shod. Sydney rode to Lyndhurst on my machine to get some books. Did some needling today.

Easter Sunday. April 2. Harry and Will drove the young mare to Chapel, put her in the trap for the first time. We all drove down with Jessie. Read *The Grandfather* to them all by the author of *Jonathan Merle*[20]. Had a letter from Louie [Barfoot] and a note from Miss May. She sent a leaf of lemon plant, it smells so sweet.

April 3rd. Easter Monday. Dull day until the evening when it was nice and bright. We all went to the Meet but Mother, Annie and Grandpa! There were lots of people there: Mr. & Mrs. Evans, Amy and Miss Ada Barnes and a little girl cousin. I was with them most of the time. Mrs. E. came down with me and Mr. E. followed and had a good view of the deer and hounds several times, and came into tea, rather fagged. Saw all sorts and conditions of men at the Meet and horses. Wrote to Miss May and described her screen for her. Two ladies called to ask the way to Burley, friends of Miss Clough's. I showed them the way. Annie and I rode our bicycles half way home with Mr. & Mrs. Evans. Annie was much better at it, not half so tired as on Friday. We met a tramp, an old man. He seemed very ill and pitiable but his breath had the wrong smell, like the Irishman who had the word "Temperance" right but not the right smell! However, we gave him some pence and I told him to go home and get some food, but he didn't go. We played at ball, catch, etc., in the afternoon until tea time. Three fellows left their machines here whilst they went after the hounds – one tandem and two cycles. Mr. Evans told us about a pony for sale at Canterton. Dad and Harry drove the young mare and went to look at it but it's not big enough. They called at Mr. Golding and bought his chestnut horse, much to Harry's delight!

April 4th. Came on to rain in the morning to my disappointment, for Sydney and I wanted to ride to Lyndhurst. Harry and Dada and Will rode after Golding's horse and got him in. Will rode Harry's young mare and she was rather skittish at the start and they went over together. Dad and Uncle and Sydney meant to go to Bournemouth today, but the weather and time did not permit. Sydney read us *Bobby Bank's Bodderment* at the supper table and we sang in the evening. Mr. Barnard came again. We started putting things straight in the rooms. Did some of the books.

April 5th. Dada and Uncle and Sidney [sic] and Dick went to Bournemouth for the day and enjoyed themselves very much. They called at Mr. Farrance's and Auntie and Mrs. Epps were just packing and starting for Bath, they are going to take the waters there. I rode to Lyndhurst and went round Stoney Cross way and called at the Gailor's to ask Tobe to come over tomorrow and look for Mills's mare with the boys. It was lovely riding with the wind and I rode to Stoney Cross in ten minutes. Went to Minstead Post Office. Willie Jeanes was there. Then I rode on to Lyndhurst and found that Mrs. Evans was out till four o'clock so I went to Mrs. Payne's and got Sydney's books and rode with Katie some way and saw Mr. F. Holloway and Miss Otten. Mr. & Mrs. Evans had Mr. and Mrs. and Miss Saul[21] to tea, so we were stiffer!! Company manners! Annie rode down and came in just as we had finished tea. When they had gone we had a nice jolly time together and saw their dog "Lassie", a Collie, such a sweet dear of a puppy! We got back just after 7 o'clock. It rained a little and came on sharp after we got home. Mrs. Evans rode a little way out of Emery

---

[19] By the American composer of popular songs, Stephen Foster (1826-64)
[20] *Jonathan Merle: West County Story of the Times* was written by Elisabeth B. Bayly: it ran to several editions, the 5th published in 1893
[21] George Frederick Saul, the Lymington ironmonger and his family

Down with us so she would get home nicely before the rain. Mr. E. was going to their Fireman's dinner; he is Secretary for them and they are to have a flare-up tonight! Got *Many Cargoes* and read the first one at the supper table. Posted parcel to Auntie. We sent for the Bible for Alf's birthday and our Centenary Farthings.

April 6. Sydney went to Lee this morning. He cycled to Lyndhurst and took train on. He is going to stay one night. It came on to rain in the afternoon. I went out and got some lovely primroses and berberry. Everything was so sweet in the rain. I did not get very wet, only damp. Tobe came over this morning and he and Harry and Willie drove the young mare and went in search of that mare of Mills' but could not find her. They have been out all day, Brockenhurst way. Wrote to Maude and Alice [Webb]. Finished putting the books right in the dining room.

April 7. Florrie's birthday[22]. Rough stormy day. Uncle Dick went to Southampton with Dad. Sydney met them in town and came home with them. Poor little Dickie is very poorly, he stayed in bed till tea time and was very queer. He is better tonight though. Mrs. Hendy is rather better. We packed Willie's bag. He is going back with Uncle[23], we are so glad he's going to have a change. Sent Maude some flowers.

[The following entry starts in Sydney's hand]

April 8th. Bee too lazy [Beatrice interlines 'busy' in brackets] to fill in the diary to day, so yours truly was privileged to do the same. She asserts she did some cooking and if she cooked the pudding for today's dinner, it was A1 and she can go on trying. Bee took me to Lyndhurst. I walked, Bee rode (my fault, not Bee's). Had tea at Shorts. Enjoyed same. Went to Mrs. Evans, gossiped (I couldn't get a word in edgeways – you know what women are) ['not' added in Bee's writing]. Called at Venvells, inspected his photography. Face the breeze and got home 7.15 (NB.B. scorched). Bee writes letters at night on foreign note paper. She seems interested (written by S. A. Kelly of L'pool).

[In Bee's hand] I forgot to put down the other evening that Harry operated on Sydney's sprouts, sad destruction! His face did resemble a scrubbing brush rather!! Great improvement in the victim. Razor blunt!!

[Sydney's hand] N.B. Slight departure from the truth in above. I was growing a beard to protect my throat but it would not take, so I shaved it with the assistance of Harry. S. A. K. [Bee's hand] Sydney *happened* to look in the glass and saw what this "beard" (?)(?) looked like so prudently resolved to take a "little off the top".

[Sydney's hand] NNBB. I can't stand this scandal so shall depart for L'pool on Monday. Say "*Au Revoir* and not Good-bye". I shall bring a razor and shaving tackle next time. [Bee's hand] (Don't rob Harry of a job Sydney!)

April 9. Sydney wrote my Diary last night for me – "variety is charming". We started to ride to Chapel, Annie, Sydney and I. At the bottom of Boldrewood Hill the chain broke on Alf's machine that Sydney was riding. He put it up in the trap and I overtook Annie and we got along nicely. The Chapel was very hot and at the end of the 3rd hymn Annie fainted. She flopped up against me and fell down in her seat. Miss Hedges came and I lifted her up and when she began to come to and Miss Hedges kindly helped her into the vestry, I on one side and she on the other. She had quite come to when we got her out of the Chapel. Then Miss H. went in to the service and we sat in the yard for 5 or 10 minutes. Then I got our machines round and we rode on gently, I pushed Annie along. Then we went to Mrs. Venvell and she gave us lemonade and biscuits!! (Sydney said he wished he had fainted too!). I played and A. laid down until the boys came and I rode Annie's machine home and Sydney rode mine. I begged of him to try Annie's but he wouldn't! Young beggar! I found the differences in the gears. It was breezy coming home. Mr. Sims sent me the names of the trees that I've tried to find out – *Juniperus Scottia* and *Juniperus Chinerais* and *Ju* [unfinished]. Read *Jonathan*

---

[22] Either Florence May's 16th birthday or Florence Kelly's 20th
[23] To Liverpool

Merle to Dickie all the afternoon. Sydney imitated Annie flopping all the rest of the day. It came on to rain a little coming home and kept on more or less all day.

April 10. Uncle and Sydney and Will went this morning at 9 o'clock. We are very sorry for them to go; we have enjoyed their visit so much, the time has simply flown. I do wish that they could have stayed longer. Uncle speaks of coming down later on in the year. Dad drove them to the station and brought me back a letter from my dear little Alice [Webb]. The first I've had from her since Xmas. They are going to take it in turns to write to me. Maude one week and Alice the next. Maude has got holidays now. Wrote to Will and we sent him some stockings we'd forgotten to pack. Harry worked the chestnut horse at bush-harrow all day; he pulls and goes splendidly. We've had a very busy day, washing day!! We sent Annie off to bed early as she is not at all well. Showery day – seasonable April Showers! I expect they have arrived at Liverpool now. I wonder if they feel fresh! I think I have written a long account tonight. Finished reading *Westward Ho*[24]. I like it very much and I "tell" it to Dick at night when he's in bed.

April 11th. Windy day, several showers but we got all the clothes dry. Mother white washed the Larder and we cleaned it out thoroughly. Mother put in the dahlias and we've saved some for Lizzie [Hendy]. I worked at my green skirt. Dada has got a nasty cut on his left arm. He was holding a piece of wood for Dick to cut with the axe, and it slipped and cut his arm badly an inch long on the outside of the arm. It aches and tinkles [sic] so. Mother had a letter from Mary, her servant at Surbiton. The first news she has heard from her for 21 years. She is married and living near the Crystal Palace. She has two children, a little boy and girl. Mother is so pleased to hear from her after many years. It's rather cold.

April 12th. Did some blue enameling, candlestick, wash stand and lamp. Made cake and tarts for my own birthday and the tarts are too hard baked; Annie left them so long. Fine day; there was quite a sharp frost last night. Mother began reading *In His Steps* to us at the supper table. My kitten is such a sweet der [sic]. Dickie made her a house in the granary which it is very proud of. He also put feathers in Ben's hair and made him a red indian. He looked so funny and sweet.

April 13. Mother white washed the ceiling of the kitchen and I washed the paint and began painting – have half done the room and I hope to finish it tomorrow. We've had a busy day. I went out in the evening and got some primrose roots and barberry of different kinds for tomorrow. Had a letter from Will, they arrived safely and he is enjoying himself. Aunt Annie wrote to mother and Annie and Grandpa and me. She is fairly well. Wrote to Maude and Alice. It has poured with rain all the afternoon it was raining [sic]. Mother wrote to Alf to go with his present and card. Mr. Cochrane's brother wrote to ask if he and his wife could come for a few days in June. We can't say for certain as we expect Mr. & Miss F[orbes]. Mr. Lambert wrote, only he and his little girl are coming.

April 14. Another wet day, heavy showers. I finished painting the kitchen. It looks nice and fresh. Did some mending, though not half as much as I wanted to do. Mrs. Evans has sent me a dear little note and ½ doz collars, only they are for habit-shirts and I don't wear that kind, it's very kind of her to think of me. I shall be 18 years old tomorrow, what a bird! I begin to feel quite ancient!! I wrote to Mr. J. G. Short and sent him a box of flowers. Sent Lizzie some dahlias and Mrs. Hendy some flowers. We sent Alf his bible but he is away and will not be back till tomorrow night. Mrs. Venvell's coming up next week. George has come, although it is so wet.

April 15th. My birthday. It has been a fine day. Mrs. Evans came up to tea and George and I rode down with her half way. George on Annie's machine, he can just reach it. Mother has given me (or promised) a white merino petticoat, some striped green muslin for a blouse, a work-basket and an old ring, Aunt Polly's old keeper, it's very thin and only fits my little finger! so I shall wear it on ties I think. Annie has given me an album for my pressed flowers. Harry and Will and Dick money for a pair of gloves and Dick has painted me a text "God is Love". He's done it very well. I've had nice letters from Auntie Polly [Chubb], Aggie, Annie, Auntie Rye [Maria Kelly] and Uncle William [Croxford], Maude and Alice, Miss M. Harris, Miss May,

---

[24] Charles Kingsley's popular novel

Louie and a text from Grandpa, so clearly written. Auntie and Uncle have sent me two patent collar studs. Aunty Polly and Aggie a substantial steel comb, Annie a book of Longfellow's poems. I began reading *Evangeline* this afternoon. All my other kind friends have promised me presents, so I have something to look forward to!! It was good of Mrs. E. to come up after all: she has taken the collars to change them if possible for me. Harry brought me in an egg that his pullet had laid for me. Mr. W. Farmers came and bought the "Freak" but he has not taken her away yet. Mrs. Hendy was about the same yesterday as last week. Sent Louie's letter at last and a line to Miss May at her wish. Louie will be home in less than a fortnight's time.

April 16th. Showery morning. Harry and I drove down his young mare to Chapel and were very late. The mare took us some minutes to get into the shafts, and then two ladies kept us waiting directing them to Burley and we were late to start in the beginning. The mare went very nicely but Harry had to hold her in with all his strength. She does go splendidly.

April 17th. [The following lines have been crossed through: Primrose Day[25]. Miss Austin is to be married today and is having a Primrose Wedding.] It has been a beautiful day. We have been working at the passage today. Mother has distempered it a tint of blue and I painted all the stone paint and began the green and after tea, Mother did some for me. I've painted full 5 hours today. Harry and Dad put Golding's horse in the trucks, he went very well. Annie finished reading the 2nd volume of Carlyle's *French Revolution*. Planted a box of forget-me-nots for Mrs. Hendy. I am wondering what Maude's "somequin" is, as it's not to make me worldly, she says!! Mr. W. Farmers came and took the cow and bought 9 pigs this morning. Mr. Barnard cycled up in his new solidly, substantial bicycle, it is a Singer and it has only had four years wear he says, but it was not manufactured 4 years ago – or 8! The pattern is slightly older than the "Modele de Luxe", the gear wheels have teeth on them fully half and innche [*sic*] at the point ⌐⌐ so!! I had a ride round the garden on it though and it's a good old crocklette! I bought a brush from Mr. Barnard today, a very nice one just in working order. He said that "I didn't know anything" because I asked him for a second-hand one. He bought ten pigs from Dad and has finished up his jobs here now.

April 18. Beautiful balmy day. Mrs. Carlion and her sister-in-law and husband called this morning to see us, the sister was a very nice bright lady and her husband a clergyman. The Fox Hounds met on the Green and they came down after the meet. Georgie and I went out this afternoon and gathered a lot of primroses to make a wreath for Tammie's [Lane] grave. It will be her birthday next Monday. I saw Mr. Lane in the wall garden, and I'm going to make it for Saturday. We met Gertie and little Daisy and a little friend out primrosing too and we gathered together. The primroses are not out in their full beauty by any means. Willie wrote to Mother and to me for my birthday. Mr. Lambert wrote two letters, one to say he *couldn't* come as the Mission was prolonged and the other to say that he *could* come after all; so he will come on Monday next. Harry rode the chestnut horse to Mr. Gulliver's after tea, he was extremely lively and graceful in his movements and bucked and jumped like – I don't know what!!! Mother was not at all well this morning so she doctored up and is better tonight. Dad and Harry are breaking the marl on the fields.

April 19. Another lovely day, quite warm or, rather, hot. Harry rode the chestnut horse to be shod and he was pretty lively. He ordered some stuff (meal) from Broomfields. Mr. Guliver's [*sic*] brother called early this morning to give Dad a message from Mr. Retford. So he rode Harry's mare across this evening and poor Mrs. Retford is feeling their discharge[26] very much. Miss Lizzie Hole and two friends came in just before tea, Mr. & Mrs. Russell, they were very nice people. Miss Hole has been here before, she is a jolly girl and has invited me to Eastbourne to stay with her. Just as we had begun tea Lizzie [Hendy] and Miss Child came in, we were so pleased to see them, it's such a long time since Lizzie came. We had a pleasant time together and I rode down as far as Emery Down with them and Annie met me coming home. I saw Mrs. Marshall and Mrs. Venvell. And Miss Harris has sent me a book for my birthday, *The Spirit of Christ*, one of Rev. A. Murray's books. Miss Duckworth has sent Grandpa some tobacco. Lizzie [Hendy] wants me to go in and

---

[25] Primrose Day was actually commemorated on the 19 April. Founded in 1883 to memorialise Benjamin Disraeli's death (1881) and to promote the Conservative principles that he espoused. The primrose was supposed to be his favourite flower. The 'Primrose Wedding' was between Hugh Evans Arkwright and Mary Catherine Austin at Lyndhurst Church on the 19 April

[26] Meaning discharge from their employment by the Hon. Auberon Herbert. The Retfords then returned to live in Ashley

stop a few days on Friday. I am going – for how long I don't know.

April 20. Had a very busy day. In the afternoon I made a wreath of primroses chiefly for Tammie Lane's grave and took it up to Mrs. Lane – she was very pleased with it. George went with me and we picked a lot of blossoms, Douglas fir and cherry blossom, barberry, etc. I wrote to Will this morning, so did Mother to let him know that he can stay a week longer. Broomfield sent up the meal this morning. Harry and Dad drove the chestnut horse in the trucks. Killed a calf, the one Dad's bought from Mr. Gulliver.

April 21. I am staying with Mr. & Mrs. Hendy and Family until Monday morning. We had a very wet morning and afternoon, but a fine evening. The drive in was bitterly cold. George came home too, we got out and ran behind the cart as it was so cold and warmed ourselves. We were very late getting in; it was 1.00 pm as we passed Millbrook Church. Lizzie and I have been shopping this evening and also to the Choir Practice. Mrs. Hendy is very poorly. Southampton is very dirty. Had a letter from Elsa this morning. Alf[27] has given me a lovely plated lamp for a birthday present, also oil and clips. Maude has not sent yet. Saw Mrs. Fred Hendy this evening and Ella, she is such a sweet derder[28]. I gave her rides on her tricycle – she is so fond of riding.

[The entry for 22 April is written in pencil.]

April 22. Cold fine day. Cooked etc., all the morning. Mrs. Hendy is very poorly again today and cannot be left. We didn't go into the cycles[29] till after tea. Liz and I went out shopping in the afternoon. She bought a dress and I got a pair of gloves, etc. I rode up to Miss Child's house after tea and had a little chat with her and her Mother, then she rode down with me and went to Jones[30] and I bought a white sailor hat. We were going out on the "Sociable"[31] but Mr. Barber got a letter from his home saying his mother was dangerously ill and he had just time to catch the last train to Salisbury. I am so sorry for him. They say he was so upset. There seems so much trouble and illness about now.

April 23. Mrs. Hendy was very bad this morning but Mr. Hendy met the Doctor and he told him what to give her and Lizzie stayed at home with her all the morning and Mary and I went to Chapel and had a very nice service. Saw Mr. Mason he is coming out when he can get a camera that he wants. A baby was christened this morning, the first Wesleyan Christening that I've seen. Constance Irene was the child's name; the poor mite howled most piteously afterwards and at the time. Lizzy and I met Miss Child and went to St. Paul's[32] with her to hear a cantata *The Woman of Samaria*[33]. It was lovely, the soloists were very good and I enjoyed it very much. Percy went too. We had tea at Miss Child's and enjoyed it. Ella, the youngest, plays the piano very well. She played *Spring Song* so nicely and several others of the *Songs without Words*[34]. We went to St. Luke's[35], their church and it *was* high. It made me feel quite unwell to see the bowing and scraping! And the sermon was not exactly helpful, twaddle! I won't become a Romanist *yet*. Postponed! Rather!!!!! We had a pleasant evening nevertheless! Saw some photos in which Trixie shone! They were chronic! Alf sang at the Baptist Chapel this afternoon. Mr. Hendy and Percy went to hear John Kensit[36]. He spoke about "Confessionals" and was splendid. We wished that we could have gone.

---

[27] Alf, *i.e.* Alfred Hendy is recorded as a motor engineer in the 1901 census and his younger brother, Percy, as a cycle and motor salesman (see biographical notes).

[28] Derder appears to be Beatrice's expression for a little darling or dear little person. Probably derived from Tame family domestic usage. Ella is Ella Constance Hendy (see biographical notes).

[29] Probably means in to Hendy's cycle shop.

[30] Probably the well-known Southampton retailing business of Edwin Jones.

[31] The Sociable was a tricycle where the riders sat side by side. For a time much favoured by couples.

[32] St Paul's, an Anglican church, was built in 1829 in London Road, Southampton. It was constructed to meet the spiritual needs of an expanding population. It was badly damaged during World War II and was demolished in 1950.

[33] *The Woman of Samaria* composed by William Sterndale Bennett (1816-75).

[34] *Lieder ohne Worte*, a group of short piano pieces composed by Mendelssohn, 1830-45.

[35] St Luke's, an Anglican church, built 1852-3 with later extensions, to serve a new parish created from St Mary's. Interestingly, the Rev. Frederick H. Bowden-Smith, of the Brockenhurst family, had been vicar there 1875-81.

[36] Listening to John Kensit (see biographical notes), whom they evidently admired, shows clearly the evangelical and non-conformist inclinations of Beatrice Tame and the Hendy family

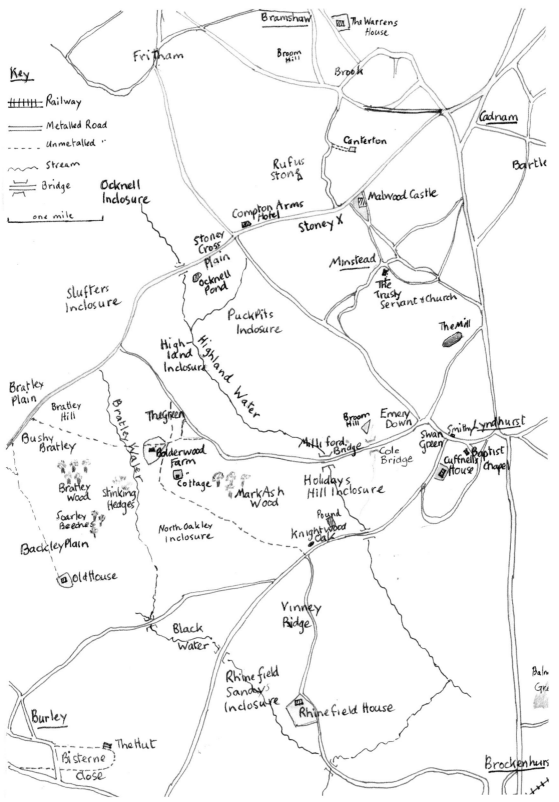

This map, drawn by Veronica Walton, shows Bolderwood and the nearby places

Tea picnic in the hayfield. Note the tea urn on the left, the horse-drawn hay rake in the background and the hobnailed boots of one of the field workers

Harvest supper at Bolderwood. Letitia Tame presides. Annie Barfoot is on the extreme left. The bearded field worker, wearing the hobnailed boots in the picnic scene, is also present

Boldrewood Farm. 1883

The original farmhouse into which Henry Tame and his family moved in 1879.
This charming watercolour sketch is by Heywood Sumner, a friend of the Tames

Old Tame.

aged 101. March 1897.

This watercolour portrait was drawn by Heywood Sumner, two years before
Beatrice penned her diary of life at Bolderwood

View of Bolderwood Farm nestling in the depths of the Forest

Brusher Mills, New Forest, Snake Catcher

F. G. O. Stuart 767

A postcard illustration of 'Brusher' Mills who visited the Tames at Bolderwood on 31 May and again on 7 June

Frederick Golden Short.
A caricature by Brewster 1915

A caricature of James Staats Forbes
by 'Spy' (Sir Leslie Ward) which
appeared in *Vanity Fair* on
22 Feb. 1900

Beatrice was a talented painter in watercolours.
This picture reveals her love of flowers which is so evident from the diary entries.
The signature reveals that it was painted after her marriage to Capt. Shaw Page

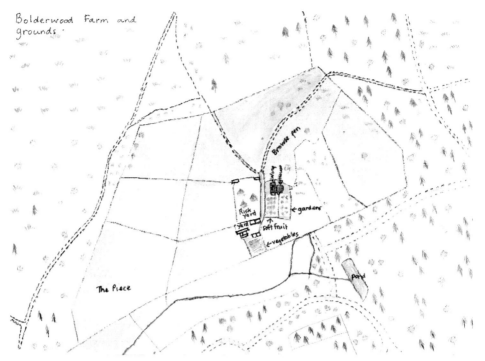

Bolderwood Farm and grounds.

Browze fern

Rick Yard

← gardens

Yard

soft fruit

← vegetables

The Place

pond

Plan of Bolderwood Farm as it was at the time of the diary. Drawn by Veronica Walton

OPEN FOREST

OPEN FOREST

OPEN FOREST

Bolderwood Grounds

a. r. p.
10 : 2 : 0

a. r. p.
1 : 2 : 19

a. r. p.
1 : 0 : 36

a. r. p.
0 : 32

a. r. p.
0 : 2 : 4

a. r. p.
0 : 1 : 31

a. r. p.
1 : 0 : 38

p.
13

a. r. p.
2 : 2 :

a. r. p.
3 : 0 : 29

a. r. p.
1 : 0 : 21

a. r. p.
2 : 1 : 34

a. r. p.
0 : 2 : 38

BOLDERWOOD GROUNDS

OPEN FOREST

BOLDERWOOD GROUNDS

BOLDERWOOD GROUNDS

Plan of Bolderwood Farm from the original lease granted to Henry Tame in 1879.
It was this small farm that occupied the lives of the family for so many years.
The lands marked 'Bolderwood Grounds' represent the area that was part of the grounds
of the extensive Bolderwood Lodge (by this date demolished) and had reverted to being forest

April 24. Have just finished up yesterday's account and it's gone 10.00 o'clock and if I don't bunk off to bed, I shan't be up before 7.00 tomorrow. I feel rather talkative or "irritative" tonight I fancy. I left East St. this morning at 10.30 and all my dear friends. Mrs. Hendy was a shade better – we had a long talk this morning. I shan't write anymore – no, *au revoir*! Alf came with me to the Station to show me the way. It was raining a little then and I came out in the same train as Mr. Lambert and Annie, and met them at Lyndhurst Road. It was pouring with rain and we got in the 'bus and came to Lyndhurst where Dada met us. It poured with rain all day long and we got very wet coming home. Annie is quite at home with us all. Harry and Dick drove the young mare to Burley and brought home the two sows. She went all right this time; on Sunday she was rather troublesome and wouldn't start once, they were driving her with a different bit. Dick rode Annie's [Barfoot] machine to Chapel. She rode home, she says she missed me pushing her up the hills etc. [The following inserted in the top margin.] Had a letter from Maude and a sweet little brooch and a book by Sheldon from Alice, *The Twentieth Door*.[37] Poor Allan has been very ill with asthma, he was better when she wrote. Maude and A. are staying with Lou to keep her company and help her. I [am] so sorry he's so unwell.

April 25. Another wet day, not so bad but very showery. I went out in the morning and got some barberry and blossoms to send to Louie and Maude and Alice. I just wrote a short note to Mormor and the little 'ousemaid. Miss A. Eyre has sent Grandpa a Memorial of Lord Nelson in the shape of a jug, in earthenware; the mouth is his cocked hat. Grandpa has given it to me for an ornament. Annie and I walked up to Mr. Lane's twice to tell them of the bicycle they want and to ask them to post some letters. I forgot the latter so we went again. Miss B. Taylor came just after dinner and we had a nice chat and I walked with her as far as Oakly [sic]. She was so pleased to see us again and we to see her. Dad and Harry drove over to Winsor to Mr. Taylor's with the chestnut horse, he went very well indeed. They put him in the trucks again tonight. Mr. Lambert has been out a good deal and I have made Annie's doll a cape and cap, etc., much to her pleasure, dear little thing, she talks away to me so freely.

April 26. Very windy today. I rode to Lyndhurst in the afternoon and got some green sateen to cover a cushion for Mrs. Hendy. Mrs. Payne is very ill and has been in bed days. The Dr says she must stay in bed 2 days more. We want her to come up to us if she can. She is thoroughly run down and is terribly weak, the noise of the traffic worries her rather too and she longs for quiet. I had tea with Mr. Evans, Mrs. Evans went home this morning for a time. She is going unexpectedly as she only made up her mind about it on Sunday. Mr. E. was gardening, sticking the peas etc. We had a talk about his schoolday battles! I found the wind stiff coming home. Called in at Mrs. Marshall's and got a letter from Auntie Parker from her. She is leaving her house for a smaller one as this one makes too much work. I wrote to Miss Harris and Uncle and Auntie Jones and sent them some flowers. I also sent a little box of flowers to Mrs. Lambert and Ruthie. Mrs. Evans had left the collars for me that are my birthday present from them, and a nice little note inside the box. They are such nice collars. Henry and Dad drove the chestnut horse to Ringwood to show him to Uncle but he was not at home so they had their drive for nothing. The horse went capitally. There was a Pony Show at Lyndhurst today as usual for every year, of the Forest Horses.

April 27. Fine day, very warm. Mr. L. walked to The Hut[38] to see Miss Robinson and Annie and I had a toy tea party to her great amusement. We went out flower gathering afterwards. Mother finished Mrs. Hendy's cushion for me and I have written to her and Lizzie and Alf. Sent off Miss Harris some flowers for her past birthday and letters. Wrote a note to Louie.

April 28. Another fine day, very tiring though. Dick and I overslept ourselves till nearly 8 o'clock when Mother came and routed us out. Sent Mrs. Hendy a large box of flowers and the cushion also a box of forget-me-nots in bloom. Sent in Alf's chain too. Dad says that Mrs. Hendy is very unwell. I did hope that she would have been better by now. Mr. Lambert rode down as far as Lyndhurst with Dad and walked back,

---

[37] The author is Charles Monroe Sheldon and this tale, running to more than 350 pages, was published by the Sunday School Union in the year of the diary

[38] The Hut was built especially for Sarah Robinson (see biographical notes) when she moved to Burley in 1892

he went into the church and saw the Fresco[39]. He brought back a letter and photo frame that had come by post to Annie from Brownie, and a Post Card for me from Annie (Bedford) asking me if I have received the parcel. I have written to her and to Auntie and Aggie tonight. Had a letter from dear Maudie. She has begun school by now and Allan is able to go out in the finest part of the day Albee is still with them. Louie and Allan, Maude stayed 10 days but duty called her home on Sunday evening! It was sweet of her to write to me, she has written Mother too and Uncle has sent two photos of Grandpa that he has had enlarged from the one Mother sent Maude.

April 29. Had a letter from Alice and a card from Louie. She is very pleased with her flowers and A. is still there. Began a letter to Eveline. Walter Farmers came over this morning. Mr. F. Tanner and Mr. Sharpe came over from Burley about Harry's horse, they stayed to dinner. Made a dress and had [sic] for Annie's doll. Mother heard from Miss May in Paris. Showery day.

April 30. Lovely warm day. Dick and I bicycled to Chapel, it was quite hot and Dick felt it very much. F. G. Short asked me to play the organ tonight as he wants to go to see Mr. Griffiths and won't be back in time for Chapel. Called at Mrs. Marshall's; saw Frank [her son, aged 19]; his Mother is very poorly and has got influenza and was in bed. Dad had a letter from Uncle Farrance. Auntie and Mrs. Epps are still at Bath, the wet weather has not helped their convalescence. Hubert Venvell came up with us for the afternoon. We had a sing in the afternoon and soon after tea we started for Chapel. Fred showed me the hymns after the service this morning, they are very pretty tunes. Hubert went to Chapel with us. We drove the chestnut mare, she goes well but won't eat corn well, so consequently she's not fat. Had a poor choir. Amy only on one side. Got on very well so I was not very nervous. Everyone said "I got on very nicely". I said inwardly "What a bit of luck"!! Hubert helped us in with the mare and saw us off, we had a pleasant drive home.

May 1. Louie and Pumpkin[40] and their respective accessories arrived this evening, for instance "tabloids" and "Buffalo Puppy". Lou looked very well but poor Pumpkin has had eczema. He is alright now but needs a bath before one can fully appreciate him. Lou has brought me a lovely pr of driving gloves for my birthday present, and Annie a sweet little gondola charm for her watch chain. I have lost my little teapot that Alice gave me. I am so sorry. Dad and Harry went over to Winsor and brought the colts home from keep, the liver coloured mare and Kitty and the Morrrrrnee. Also the mare that we are to try to drive about and to be reliable for us. Helped Dickie in the yard a little last Satur. 22nd and 24th all four sows went to Burley (memo for Dad). Walter Farmers came this morning and bought 7 more pigs (F 9^{S}B.1^{S}2)[41]. Mother had a letter from Will, he has been to the Isle of Man on Jack's vessel and is enjoying himself exceedingly. He says he will probably start on Wednes. and get home on Friday. Uncle Dick has written too, he says if Will's health improves he'll come, it depends on that!!

May 2. Painted the insides of the passage doors green. Wrote the end of my letter to Eveline and posted it and some flowers to Auntie Pollie and our letters. Mr. Lambert and Annie and I had a picnic amongst the beeches at the bottom of the B[olderwood] Hill. It was so pleasant and the place was lovely. I gave Annie a swing on a bough. I rode on to Lyndhurst and my chain made such a noise that I got off and tightened the chain. I could not do it properly so went on to Mr. Venvell and he did it for me with his plyers [sic]. Saw Hubert. Called on Mrs. Payne, she had been up for a short time in her room today and feels better. She is coming up for a couple of days tomorrow week if she is well enough. Bought some hat varnish, navy blue, and a tiny doll and button hook and boxes for Ruthie and Annie and Freddie. I have dressed the dolls for Annie and made it a dolly *for the* dolly, in its arms. Miss Hillar rode a short way with me but would not face the Swan Hill. Saw Frank and Tom Lane and had a chat with them as we were coming home.

May 3. Went on putting the room straight. Mr. Lambert and Annie went at noon. They both said that it is the happiest holiday that they've had, we are so glad, they both looked much better and Annie was quite

---

[39] This is the famous, large reredos fresco painted by Frederic Leighton in 1862, though twice restored in the 20th century, remains as an artistic masterpiece and major draw for visitors to Lyndhurst. It depicts the parable of the Wise and Foolish Virgins (Matthew, 25).

[40] Pumpkin is May Forbes's pet dog.

[41] This formula appears to mean: F = fattening, B = breeding and the superscript s = sows.

rosy and jolly. Harry drove them down with the fresh mare and she went well, and he had her shod, she has been running wild all the winter. Mother cut out my new petticoat and we began to make it. My teeth began aching at tea and got worse later; I've got a gathering[42] I think. Went off to bed early as I couldn't do much and had a ginger plaster, so far so good! We sent Annie some flowers for the 5th.

April 4. [*sic*] These two days have been much colder. Neddy Compton came over. Dad had cards from Mr. Evemy and Mr. Wells. The tuner will come on Monday and Mr. E. says there is a mare in Kingston Pound[43] which he thinks is ours. Harry and Dad drove the little mare over and found the mare was Harry's – 12/- to pay. Harry walked all the way home. I put my side saddle on the fresh mare and rode her for the cows, she goes very well indeed and is quite quiet. Helped Dick milk and do the work. The heifers did not come so I saddled the mare again and went for them. I rode her astride that time and it was much nicer. She has a small trot and shakes rather with the side saddle. Went round with the gun but had no chance of a shot so came in and wrote a letter to Miss May, from Pumpkin for a lark, have tried to describe his feelings in his puppy way. My face is very swollen tonight, it's ached more or less all day and increased in size.

May 5. Annie's (Bedford) birthday today. Mother sent her a marked testament and one of Grandpa's photos, the large ones, the other day. Harry's mare had a mare colt this morning. He led her all the way from Kingston Pound yesterday. The colt is a very nice one but rather poor. Harry went out this evening and found Woodford's mare has a ˣcolt, horseˣ. Neddy Compton came and ground his turf spade[44] and had some lunch. He told Harry about the colt. I went for the cows again, on the same mare. I like that work! It is lovely to ride again. The Forest is lovely. Both yesterday evening and this evening the sunsets have been lovely. I found the cows in the bottom below the Elk[45] tree and it all looked beautiful with the bog myrtle all in bloom. Helped milk as Harry cut his finger – the hay knife fell on his hand. We finished my new petticoat. Mrs. Hendy is better this week, I am so glad.

May 6. Had letters from Annie and Ruthie and Aggie, such funny notes, all of them. Dad had a letter from Willie. He starts tonight at 6 o'clock tonight and arrives Padstow in Cornwall on Monday[46] and comes through Salisbury to Southampton in the evening. The wind is very cold today. I rode for the cows, had a long ride before I met them at the top of Bratley Hill coming from Slufters. I started at about 5 o'clock and did not get home till 7.30. Harry's liver coloured mare had a nice horse colt this evening. Mr. Baynes has written about

Cows belonging to the Tames grazing at Bushy Bratley

the horse to Dad and he has replied. Louie finished making the blinds and I trimmed my hat with the bright blue ribbon Dad bought me yesterday. I saw 5 deer in Bratley this evening[47] – they looked so pretty. Alf has come out on his bicycle, not on motor power. Mrs. Hendy is getting up a little each day now. Wrote to Maude and Alice.

May 7. Annie, Alf, Harry and I rode to Chapel and Dick rode Annie's machine home and she drove home. We stayed to Communion. Louie, Annie and I and Dad walked home. Mr. Scamell has asked for letters

[42] See note 11, above.
[43] This pound for stray animals was situated at Kingston, just south of Ringwood.
[44] A spade with a pointed blade and a curved handle, designed for cutting the turves in the New Forest.
[45] Elk, according to the *OED* and Halliwell's *Dictionary of Archaic Words* is a kind of yew tree from which the wood for bows is taken. Or it could be just a phonetic spelling for oak.
[46] This refers to a sea voyage from Liverpool to Padstow taking over 24 hours to complete.
[47] The diary is written 48 years after the Deer Removal Act of 1851 and the reference illustrates that the deer were re-establishing themselves in the Forest.

from 10 communicants to promise to stay every Sunday in the morning, except once a month, and have a weekly celebration. A lady and gentleman came this afternoon, Germans from Berlin, they were very nice, refined people. They had come from Bournemouth for the day and hired from Brockenhurst St[ation]. We gave them some tea and they were so pleased, they have invited me to go and see them in Berlin, Mr. & Mrs. Oscar Hahn. Mrs. Hahn is so pretty. They are coming to see us again. Alf and Harry walked to Burley with Sprite. Alf was going to ride Golding's horse but he threw him off; his foot hatched-up in the stirrup and he had a very narrow escape from serious injury. Dick and Dad and I went for a little walk.

May 8. Harry drove Jesse down to be shod and to meet the tuner, Mr. Burgess, but he came by an earlier train and walked up. He tuned Miss May's piano and ours and mended the note of the harmonium that had gone wrong. I drove him down in the afternoon with the little mare, had tea with Mrs. Venvell. She has given me a photo of herself and ½ doz. nice handkerchiefs for a birthday present, it is kind of her to think of me. Mrs. Pontifex and a friend called and wanted to see the pictures. They were bicycling. We gave them a cup of tea for which they were grateful as they had lunched on sandwiches, and the tea was "Homelea". Alf went this morning as usual about 9.0. We had a wire from Willie from Padstow. He is coming home tomorrow; he has been away a month today.

May 9. Finished getting Miss May's rooms ready. I dusted the whole place, pictures and all and put flowers and I have arranged 28 vases this evening. I went out soon after tea and got a lot of crab apple blossom, it is most sweet and looks lovely. Had a nice long letter from Eveline. My teeth are rather queer tonight. Harry and Dada rode to Godshill to see Mr. J. Witt's mare, they like her very much, but she rears up and won't go in harness well. They saw another mare too and she was good. Had a telegram from Miss May this evening to say that she will be here tomorrow evening. Feel very tired tonight. It

The new calf

is 10.15 p.m. and Willie has not turned up yet. I hope nothing has happened to injure him in any way. Cherry has got a nice bull calf.

May 10. Harry went over to Mr. Taylor's on Willie's bicycle early this morning about this mare. Dad doesn't want to have her now she is so shaken. He has gone over again this evening and taken her back. We were all feeling anxious about Willie as he was to come last night. He has come now looking brown and well. He has walked up from Lyndhurst; he could not get away yesterday but got from Padstow to Fremington [Devon] yesterday and met Mr. Morris there and stayed the night. He came as far as Salisbury with him and then changed and came on to Eastleigh and Southampton West. He has had a lovely holiday thanks to kind friends and the country is beautiful he says. How I should love to go to Cornwall and Devon etc. Miss May and Miss Bingham have come, they arrived about 8 o'clock. I dressed Pumpkin up with streamers of pink paper and a bunch of Honesty on his noble brow and took him up the hill to meet them. He looked so cracked and we all roared with laughter – he was so mad and excited. Miss May has brought lovely china cups and saucers and heaps of beautiful things; we are going to have a rare unpacking tomorrow. Miss

May Forbes. A photographic portrait by Frederick Golden Short

30

Bingham has brought her bicycle and they are both delighted with the place and to come again. I made some meringues for a surprise for Miss May's dinner and they have turned out very fairly, they both said they were lovely!! I am so glad, for they are tender things to manage. Cut out 3 calico garments, so I shall have heaps of work. Topsy has got a colt.

May 11. Miss May rode to church early this morning. I lent her my bicycle and she liked it very much. The Postboy wheeled Miss May's "Singer" up for her. Mrs. H. has kept it very well. Miss May and Miss Bingham and Louie unpacked all the groceries and china, such heaps of rice and sugar!! The things are bought rather indiscriminate as to quantitys [*sic*]! Dad and Harry drove Golding's horse to Ringwood and sold him to Uncle and Harry bought Uncle's Joey. Uncle sent me some nice polyanthus and cauliflowers and daisies. Had a letter from Maude. She is feeling better now she is at home in the mornings. Miss Bingham has brought her mandoline [*sic*]– we tried a piece this evening *Beauty's Eyes* – Miss May singing.

[The following line and half in pencil.] *May 12.* Miss May and Miss B. rode to Lyndhurst and did some shopping. Arthur and Tobe Gailor called and wanted to help catch some mares. Mrs. Hendy is better this week. Dad took my little kitten to Miss Mason and it must have got out on the way. The horse was troublesome at Chandlers and Dad thinks that she must have jumped out on him. I do hope the dear little mite will get a home. Wrote to Maude and Alice a good long letter.

May 13. Did all the birthday cooking this morning, had a fair turn at it. Will and Sydney have got me a Veeder Cyclometer[48] for my machine, it is good of them to think. Auntie has sent Mother a suet cutter by Willie. I rode to Lyndhurst after tea. Started at 6.0 and bought a green and brown shot moreen[49] petticoat for Mother to give Annie on Tues., and a pair of brackets from Will and I and a box of Fancy Note[paper] for Harry to give her. I bought and gave Mrs. Marshall a little bracket too. It is her birthday[50] today and no one had remembered her. She gave me some lovely gillyflowers. Saw Mrs. Payne, she gets about but her back is so bad. Saw Mrs. Evans too she was with Miss Hedges at the window and they beckoned me up, so we had a small talk and Mrs. E. came with me to Miss Hilliars. Poor Miss. Hedges has been so poorly and is now – has no appetite at all. She looks so ill. Mr. A. Duckworth wrote to Grandpa to say that he and his 2 daughters and son-in-law are coming to see him on Monday. Miss May gave me several nice blouses and a white coat and skirt. Met Amy at Mrs Payne's she is going for her holiday soon to Cranley[51].

May 14. Morning breezy and fine but wet in the afternoon. Miss May, Miss Bingham and Willie, Dick and I cycled down. I pushed Miss May up all the hills such as they are! *i.e.* stiff enough when you are working doubly hard. Willie helped Miss B. half-way. Dad drove down to fetch them home as it began raining and they had got their best hats on and were taking lunch with the Austins and just as he got there they were starting in a fly and so he had a drive for nothing. They came to tea and we sang all the evening. Mr. Tregold called.

May 15. Rev. and Miss Duckworth and Mr. & Mrs. Smith came on horseback to see Grandpa. Rev. D. is the son of his [Grandpa Tame's] last master. They stayed to tea and we gave them two of Grandpa's photos. [The remainder of this day's entry is written in pencil.] The gentlemen were very genial and pleasant but the ladys [*sic*] were so stout and plain and rather shy. The coachman came too. He walked over to take charge of the horses and Harry and Will drove him back to Stoney Cross, they are staying at the Compton's Arms, they wanted to drive the horse. Mother is very unwell, she was so giddy this morning that she couldn't stand, so dosed herself and lay down a little time. It is a bad bilious attack and sickness. She has hardly been able to do anything or eat at all today. I don't feel very well, my throat is sore and nasty. Annie has got a tooth gathering and is suffering a good deal of pain.

---

48 Veeder Cyclometer for measuring the mileage covered by a bicycle was invented in 1895 by Curtis Veeder, founder of the Veeder Manufacturing Company in Bristol, Connecticut, USA
49 A stout corded fabric of either wool or cotton.
50 Her 66th birthday.
51 Cranleigh, Surrey, rather than Cranley, Suffolk.

May 16. Annie's birthday. Louie has given her a pr of large framed texts, and we [opened?] the presents I got on Saturday and my first lamp, an enamelled one, now I have a plated one, I can dispense with it!! Brownie sent her a nice little double ink stand and letter. Miss May and Miss Bingham came to tea and in the evening Miss B. brought her mandoline and Miss May her songs and we had a very pleasant evening. We had a go at Scott Gally's songs altogether. I'm now writing this up [the sentence is incomplete and there follows eight unused lines].

May 17ᵗʰ. All rather better today, though my cold is nasty. Mrs. Austin came up to tea with Miss May. She was late as she had a puncture on the way. It is very windy. Tobe and Arthur Gailor came this morning and they and Harry and Willie went out for the Topsy family – some of the wildest mares in the Forest. The[y] met with a man named Mr. Tuck and he lent them one of his horses and Harry rode. They got them near the Sanatorium[52], brought them home and printed them and all had a good tea. Miss May made a seed cake today. It is so good, she is delighted. Annie sent Brownie some flowers, it is her birthday tomorrow.

May 18ᵗʰ. It is very rough and windy with occasional showers. Mr. Mason and Rosie cycled from Southampton this morning for the day. Rose is staying for a week; we've asked her to stop now that she is here. Will rode down this morning and got some Epsom Salts for the calf that is so ill. Mr. Mason has gone home. It is very windy but he has got the wind in his back. Harry drove to Emery Down and Miss May started with him to fetch her bicycle back but met Mr. Forbes and Mr. Fleet on the way. She had read the letter carelessly and did not take in that the day was altered as we expected them on Friday. Rose and I were out flower gathering and came in to find Mr. Fleet here, and the carriage, and that Mr. F. and Miss May were walking and would be in soon. We had such a scurry to get up a dinner and make up 3 fresh beds. Had a nice letter from Auntie Pollie.

May 19. Dick rode Rosie's bicycle in, as Sue wants it. Miss May and her father were unable to go out this evening because it rained so. Rose and I went to see how the lilies are growing, they will be out in about a week's time. Uncle Farrance wrote, Auntie and Mrs. Epps are coming home. Harry is unable to go for Joey because of the rain. Books came. Kitty has got a nice mare colt.

May 20. Very windy day and showers occasionally. Harry drove Dad's chestnut mare to Ringwood and brought Joey back for Miss May to drive and left the mare for Uncle. They did not like parting with him at all and were both upset, they are so fond of him. Poor Harry had an unpleasant job. Auntie [Farrance] and Mrs. Epps are both better for their change. Harry and Will drove down for some oats to Mr. Venvell's and I went with them to fetch Miss Bingham's bicycle from Mrs. Austin's; it runs very easily but the saddle was uncomfortable and I felt like slipping over the back of the saddle, it was so high at the point. Saw Mr. Evans, he's got a cold. We stopped at Mrs. Venvell's and she and Mrs. Allan are coming up on Monday if it's fine. Harry had a letter from Hubert, he is better in health. The chestnut horse is rather lame again. Yesterday and [*sic*] elderly lady and gentleman called to see Grandpa and gave him 6d. and 6-pennyworth of coppers when they said goodbye to him!! He took it and they are "two of the elect"!!!

May 21. Whit Sunday. Annie and Dick and I rode to Chapel. Dick on Miss Bingham's machine, she rode in the trap. Miss May went to church[53] early. Annie got on very well. Grandpa had a letter from poor Mrs. Gilbert, she is in bed and so ill. They have been expecting mortification to set in, her legs are bad. It was kind of her to write. It was a very damp all the afternoon, a dusty rain. I read to Rose and Dickie.

May 22. Whit Monday. Have had a fairly busy day and enjoyed it very much, tho' I am tired now after it. Our first visitor was Fred Clark, he left his machine here all day and came down after lunch and played cricket. And a Mr. Wellman walked down whom we have never met before, and played with us, Mr. Fleet and he shone! *We* were all quite middling. Fred brought his sister and 6 friends down to see Grandpa after tea and he and his friend tried to put my new "Veeder" on but failed in getting it right – it works backwards,

---

[52] The Sanatorium at Linford had been recently built by Dr Reginald M. Smyth, then aged 31, a young physician from Wolverhampton. He suffered from tuberculosis, himself. In 1901 the Sanatorium was described in the census as a 'Private institution for the treatment of consumption', it then accommodated 16 patients.

[53] Probably Christchurch, Emery Down

they are most kind to do it for me. Harry drove to Emery Down and brought Mrs. Venvell and Mrs. Allan up and Mr. Venvell drove up afterwards and brought his camera and took us all in a group and Dad and Mother alone and me alone on my bicycle. It was an awful feeling and I am longing to see what I look like! I'm sure I shall look —- well!! peculiar!!! Mr. Macpherson and Mr. Cleveland came and Georgie. Mr. M. came down after tea and had a wash and brush-up. They all came with a party so we did not have them all the time. Rene is very poorly, her tonsils are so bad. We had several heavy showers in the morning but in the afternoon it cleared up and was lovely. I held Mr. Forbes up on a bicycle this morning for a short distance, he's actually begun to learn to ride, it was lovely. He was rather nervous. I did not think he would trust *me* to hold him up!! Miss Bingham went for a ride. We walked up to Lanes [at Bolderwood Cottage] with Fred, the boys and Rose and I.

May 23. Mr. and Mrs. Mason arrived just before 12 o'clock after a windy ride. Mr. Mason went on at the trap, he is most kindly varnishing it and making it fresh and nice. Rev. and Mrs. Hughes[54] came to lunch with Mrs. F. and Miss May; she went to meet them with Harry and Joey in the 4 wheeler. Rev. Mr. & Mrs. Chadband S. P. came unto us empty and went home *full*. Note by Harry!!!! [The sentence was written by Harry.] – short but sweet. Mr. *i.e.* King "Emery"! & Mrs. Emery and their daughter came in this afternoon and stayed to tea, whilst at tea, Mrs. Appley and her brother-in-law came in and they had tea too. They wanted a photo of Grandpa to put in the *Graphic*. He is getting quite noted! Rose and I rode as far as Queens Road [Lyndhurst] with Mr. & Mrs. Mason and called on Mrs. Evans and had a chat; she has got 3 people staying there. Miss Hedges was there. We had a very pleasant ride. Called at Shorts and got Mrs. Evans' parcel for Annie. It is a pretty brass ['inkstand' deleted] watch stand. Poppet had a colt, a mare, last night. [The remainder of the day's entry written in Harry's neat hand.] (Facts by the Fairy) I'm afraid Mr. Chadband's anticipations were doomed to a certain amount of disappointment, expecting to have a glorious bust out of the wine that comes from the fair Province of Champagne, he for once made sure of his chickens before they were hatched, and he had to be contented with the wine that was made in Germany. Harry, who was never so happy as when fetching and taking back the Rev. gentleman and his wife, was highly entertained and greatly edified by a full and particular description of that gentleman's pedal extremities, and on arrival at the glorious Cross-crowned dwelling[55], the soft and soapy one tumbled out of the trap, put his hands into his pockets and *kept them there* (If Harry had any anticipations they were also knocked on the head).

May 24. Very wet day. It has been raining steadily all the evening and still there's more to follow. The Hon. Gerald Lascelles[56] and Mr. Howard, Commissioner of Woods and Forests, called to see Dad. Miss Bingham has broken her brake somehow so I have taken it off and down [sic] it up and written a note to Alf to get it repaired. Miss May and Mr. Forbes have not been able to get out today.

May 25. Mr Forbes and Mr Fleet went back, leaving here at 1.30. Miss May went in the carriage to Brockenhurst St[ation] and her Clipper machine had been sent back by Miss M. Ayles and she rode it home and called on two old ladies there. The front wheel is not straight and it's rather groggy altogether and wants overhauling. Miss F[orbes] took Miss B's brake down to Lyndhurst but could [not] get it mended. Mrs. Hughes came up; she drove up with an old lady and is staying a couple of nights here. Made some more meringues, they were only fair, and the oven was a bother, I couldn't get it the right heat. Rose and I went up to the lilies and found 5 in bloom and lots coming on, we went out just before dark and got lots of laburnum and other flowers. Had a very busy day.

May 26. Rosie went home with Dada. Have sent in Miss May's bicycle's head screw to get another, the nut is soft and rounded and I can't tighten up the handlebar. Miss Bingham and I were going to Rufus Stone but went to Lyndhurst, as Dick let the 'Clipper' [fall] over that she was to ride and broke the guard and bent the brake so I took the guard of[f] and rode the machine down and Miss B. rode mine. I had [to] wait for 2 hours whilst it was done, forks straightened and brake and a piece put on to the guard. We went into

---

[54] The vicar of Emery Down and his wife
[55] The vicarage at Emery Down (though no longer used as such) still retains the terracotta cross crowning the gable.
[56] Deputy Surveyor of the New Forest, 1880-1915

the Church and Miss B. rode home. I made a series of calls and saw lots of my friends. Mrs Cheeseman gave me a delicious cream rose which I gave to Mrs. Evans. Mrs. Payne is coming up on Monday evening to stay till Wednesday. Had tea with Mrs. Evans and Katie was there to tea as well, so we had a jolly time. Mrs. E. is coming up on Monday if her people go. Called at Mrs. Venvell's and they gave me three photos; mine is so good and the group is splendid, all except Dick and I and we've moved in one slightly. Mother and Dada are both laughing very much. Dad saw Mrs. Hendy for the first time since she's been ill and she made him promise to let me go in on Saturday but it is not manageable so I'm here writing up this record at 8 p.m. Saturday evening as I didn't get time yesterday. Miss May and Mrs Hughes went to Portsmouth to see the little boy[57], he is 13 on Sunday. They drove Joe down to the St[ation] and back.

Satur. [*May 27*]. Now for today's doings. Before breakfast I had a regular turn at bicycle repairs, fixed Miss B's brake and guard and put on my carrier which I've lent her and fixed up a new parcel affair over the back wheel that she bought yesterday and did various things to the three wheels. They all three started at about 9 o'clock, cycling to the St[ation] to go to Trent[58] for a few days, till Tuesday. Mr. Ing's came. Dad paid Harry's mares' keep yesterday. Mrs. Lambert wrote a very nice letter. Had a turn at tid[y]ing up my blouses and fronts etc. It has been a lovely day, a little cold though. Auntie Kelly sent a card to say that she can't come today, we are hoping to see her later on.

May 28. I rode to Chapel alone and played the harmonium[59]. Will rode down later and we came home together. Lilie May came back with us and Dick and I went down with her and Dickie to meet her father and Florrie as they were coming to meet her halfway. I wheeled Lilie on Annie's machine and Dick coasted on mine, met Mr. May and Florrie at the Cole Bridge[60] and Mr. May was quite willing for Lily to stay the night, so I wheeled her back part of the way – she can nearly ride. Harry and Willie drove to Winsor after the liver coloured mare and the Mornee and found them at Money Hills and brought them home; they had tea with Mr. Taylor. Mrs. Seward wrote to H[arry] to say they would come the next fine day.

May 29. Mr. and Mrs. Pope and Mrs. Seward turned up at dinner time and stayed the rest of the day. Mrs. P. laid down to go to sleep but failed, she was feeling very queer, she is a great sufferer. Whilst we were at tea a strange lady and gentleman drove in, friends of Uncle Willie's from Lea, they had tea with us and were very pleasant and nice; they came to see Grandpa specially. I took them round the place and they were charmed with everything!! I wheeled Lily on my bicycle to meet Florrie, met her this side of Milliford [sic] and walked to the Cole Bridge and Flo rode my machine. Turned back and met Mr. and Mrs. P. and Mrs. Seward and rode to E[mery] Down with them and went to Post. At 9 p.m. Mrs. Payne came walking down, carrying her bag, they had driven her up to the Green. We had just welcomed her when Alf and Lizzie Hendy came in Mr. Warr's motelle(?). We heard the bunk! bunk! bunk!! from afar! We were surprised, they seem to "be all coming". They have been talking about Marchwood, this farm that is for sale. Had a very busy, rushing day altogether.

May 30. Mr. Golding the rate collector came and his son, Ted, in the morning. Mrs. Payne rested all the morning chiefly and would go home after dinner so Dad and Harry took her down with them on their way to Marchwood. They met Alf there and saw the place but it's rough – a second Thorney Hill and the land cold and poor so that plan is stopped. About 9.30 Mr. and Mrs. Richard Light and a friend and Mrs. L's mother, they were a queer party and all had tea – they had driven over from Totton in a ['fly' deleted] cab. The old lady has been ill. I just got the dusting [done in] Miss May's rooms before she and Miss Bingham came. They have had a lovely time at Trent and Miss Mary Ann Brookes is coming ['tomorrow' deleted] on Thursday for 2 nights.

---

[57] This is Sidney, son of the Rev. Herbert Hughes who had become a cadet in the Royal Navy.

[58] There is no indication as to which Trent this might be. Trent in Dorset is possible. The nearest station to it is at Yeovil Pen Mill, though from Southampton Sherborne would be more convenient.

[59] This harmonium had been bought new for the Baptist chapel in 1859.

[60] Cole Bridge is about 400 yards east of Milliford Bridge

May 31. The weather is lovely and so hot, summer seems to have begun in earnest. I rode to meet Mrs. Macpherson who came out for the day. I went in to Mrs Payne's and got some lace for my dress. Saw Mrs. Evans. I met Mrs. M. on the station road, very hot indeed, we took it very gently coming home and called at Mrs. Venvell's and had some lemonade. Brusher[61] brought two gentlemen here for some milk and showed us his adders, etc. The gentlemen showed us a moth that we'd not noticed, the bee hawk, just like a bumble bee, it hovers round the ['laburnum' deleted] azalias and rhododendrons. Mr. and Mrs. Lane and Beata and Alice came directly after dinner, so we had quite a tea party. Mr. Macpherson came about 6 o'clock and we all had tea out of doors for the first time – it was so nice. I sent my letter to Maude and some flowers. Strawberry heifer had a calf. We have all had a pleasant day and after tea we had a cushion fight. Miss May and Miss B. drove to Lyndhurst. Letter from Auntie Kelly. She is not coming.

June 1. Quite a summer's day. Dick and I drove over to Winsor to fetch Mrs. Seward over, we drove Joey, he went very well. Called at Mr. Taylor's and took Mrs. Taylor a rabbit and *Family Friend* to read, they were at tea. We left home at 4.00 and got there at about 5.30. Called at Mrs. Venvell's and took her some cream for tea and told Mr. V. that Harry would meet him at Fritham at 9.00 next morning. Called at Gailor's too and asked for Tobe to come over: saw Mr. Gibbons [*sic*], Miss G. had gone to Brockenhurst to have a puncture mended. We had tea at Mrs. Pope's and stayed for a short time. Mrs. P. gave me some violet roots and french lavender slips and two sweet little crimson roses to wear and a bit of azalia. Enjoyed the drive immensely, it was such a lovely evening.

June 2. Gailor did not come so Dick went with Harry to Whiteparish to take Woodford's young mare and the Mornee to keep, they met Mr. Venvell and Mr. Inwood there and Harry came home partway, to Fritham with Mr. Venvell and Dickie rode the brown mare "Merry". Wrote to Lizzie for the footrests for Miss Bingham and she never sent them. Helped Willie milk etc., and do up the work, it was 9.30 when we'd done out of doors, then I came in and played *Beauty's Eyes* for Miss May and Miss B. and several other things. Will turned the turf, Dick and Harry left home at 7.30 or 8.0 and didn't get home till after 10 – they're tired out. I have got another cold, it makes me hoarse. The heat tries Mrs. Hendy very much. Alf was off to London to fetch down a motor. Mrs. Seward and I got a lovely lot of lilies in Puck Pits. Mrs. Egerton and her son, the Rev. George Egerton, came to see Grandpa and had tea.

June 3. These last few days have been intensely hot. Mrs. Seward is staying till Monday, she has written home to her Father and Harry posted the letter at Burley tonight when he took the sow. The farm that they were talking of and went to see on Tuesday was sold for £900 (22 a[cres])– [inserted vertically into the margin: 'Twiggs Lane end Farm'] and Testwood fetched £1,650 (24 a.) – too much for Alf and the boys. Miss May and Miss Brookes and Miss B. went for a picnic at Berry Wood; yesterday they spent the day at Bournemouth. Miss Brookes fell getting out of the carriage, Joe moved and she jumped. I rubbed her knees well and that relieved her but she is so stout and falls heavy so it shook her. Miss Robinson sent Grandpa a box of sweets and Mrs. Retford wrote to Mother. No visitors today for a wonder. Lots of turbulent feelings.

June 4. A very hot day, Will and Dick and I rode to Chapel. Harry drove Miss May down early to S[unday] Sch[ool] with his bit of 'Gold-dust' and all the others came in the light cart. We had to hurry going down as we were late and it was awfully hot. Read to Dick and had a nap in the afternoon. Miss May stayed to lunch at the Vicarage [Emery Down] and took Mrs. Hughes' class as she is not well and walked up to tea with us, we had tea out of doors and I went for a walk with Mrs. Seward, Miss Bingham and Miss Brookes. We had some singing. Willie and Harry sang together.

June 5. Miss May and Miss Bingham went to a Flower Service at E[mery] Down Church and had tea at Mrs. Hughes'. Louie and I went to the farthest plot of lilies and there we found only one [in] flower, we found a nice little lot. Pumpkin went off hunting rabbits and did not come back for ever so long. I went with Miss May and Miss B. to look for him, it was dark and when he came he had a good hiding. Mrs. Seward was

---

[61] Harry 'Brusher' Mills (see biographical notes).

anxious as they did not come for her till late, she was afraid they would not come, but Mr. and Mrs. Pope drove over and just caught them going over the Green in time to say goodbye. Got lily roots for Mrs. Forbes' grave and Miss Brookes and flowers for Miss Bingham and anemones, hydranger [*sic*], narcissus and Cuttings.

June 6. Miss May and Miss Brookes and Miss B. all went early this morning. Harry drove his mare to the St[ation] with the luggage. I rode Miss B's bicycle and they drove Joey. Called at Mrs. Marshall and took her a few flowers – she gave me some too and some ginger beer. I was so hot and dry, the heat was intense, no breeze, I "scorched" along, in one sense of the word! Drove Joey back. Had a nice letter from Maude, they were still at Louie's as she and Allan and Arthur had gone to Bedford. Lou sprained her ankle; fell from her machine when coasting. Ruthie Lambert wrote to tell me that she has another little brother. Went out with the gun but had no chance of a shot. Harry had his mare shod. Miss Brookes has given us all cordial invites to Trent.

June 7. Hot, with a slight breeze. Went out with the gun again and after mouching[62] round till dusk Dad told me to go out by the bottom gate and I did and shot a nice young rabbit! I really did not expect to kill, but I did, what a bit of luck!! Harry went to Mr. Taylor's to get his new trap. Annie bicycled to Lyndhurst and took tea with Mr. Short, but was too late for shopping as the shops were closed. Mrs. Evans had gone out for a picnic with Mrs. Holly. Mr. and Mrs. Baily brought up the coal and had tea; their little boy and the "Mrs." came for a treat, the boy was a derder. Meant to do a lot of needlework but went shooting instead, I'm sorry to say! We sent flowers to Mrs. Worrall. Brusher and those two gentlemen came again.

June 8. Colder today. Gave Mother a bicycle lesson this evening, she got on very well indeed! Got up at 4.30 a.m. and got the gun and mouched round till 6.00 – only got one chance of shooting and bossed or was too far away. Came in and had a cup of tea with Dad and the boys and took the others some in bed. Have been out again tonight, shot once but took too long a range, I just chanced it, so all I've got today is an empty barrel! it is disappointing, but everyone must have their bosses, I suppose! Made a collar and bow for Mary Hendy of pink satin edged with a ruche of white chiffon. Have written her a note and got heaps of flowers. Very little needlework done again. Mother sent some flowers to Auntie Rye.

June 9. Mother went down with Dad and I rode to Mrs. Marshall's to meet her this morning and after resting with her we came home and I gave Mother a lesson on the way. We saw two gentlemen coming at one part of the ride and I wouldn't let Mother get off. It was Mr. Fred Short and a friend, he wished he had got another plate in his camera and was surprised at seeing Mother mounted so. Mr. Goff and some men came this morning, Miss May met Dad at Hendy's and had tea with them and Lizzie went with her to buy an American organ, she says it is a beauty. Miss May drove home with Dada and has enjoyed her time in London. Mother had a letter from Miss Robinson, she wants to know Grandpa's Christian name.

June 10. I went with Miss May to the St[ation] this morning. I rode her machine from Mrs. Hughes' to the St[ation] and when we got to Lyndhurst we found there was not time to catch the train at Lyndhurst Rd., so she drove to Brockenhurst and I rode out to Lyndhurst Rd. and took her hat box and bicycle by train and met her at B[rockenhurst]. and drove home from there, saw Amy, she only came home yesterday and her Aunt was going then. Mr. Marchant says he's coming next Saturday. I wonder if it's true! I did not take the washing home, so this evening I have been down on my crocklette to despatch a nightdress to Miss May and fetch home collars and fronts for Dad and the boys. I had a stiff pull to Lyndhurst Rd. as the wind was in my face so. Had a nice letter from Mary Hendy thanking me for the collar and wanting me to come in for a week, but I can't. Had a letter from Miss Bingham and Grieg's latest pieces – *Lyric Pieces* and I'm longing for a practice at them. It is so kind of her to send them to me. And to Annie muslin for a skirt and Ellen 3 nice handk[erchie]fs.

---

[62] The more usual spelling is mooching (mooch and mooched).

June 11. Will and I rode to Chapel. Letters from Mr. Wells and Mr. King. Had a nice walk, Lou, Dick and I, and we threw Pumpkin in the stream several time[s] to cool him down. The organ gave up the ghost in the last hymn so we all sang without it.

June 12. Drove Joey down to fetch Mr. J. Short up for day. I found that Joe had one shoe off in front soon after I started so I could not get on very fast. I had two shoes put on him whilst I walked into Lyndhurst. I think Mr. Short thought I was not coming. I did my shopping, got chiffon for my hat and got the books, the[n] Mr. S. walked up with me to the Blacksmiths, put the horse in and drove home. Mr. S. has not been up for 30 years and I do hope he has enjoyed himself, his asthma is so bad. We looked at the pictures and Miss May's photos etc., all the afternoon and Harry drove him down. They

Sharpening the scythes

started back at 6.00. Mr. Short brought Mama and me a little bottle of Vinolia Lavander [sic] Water. He is such a dear old gentleman. Mr. W. Holloway called in just as they were starting and had some tea and a talk with them. Harry cut Will's arm this morning when helping him put his scythe on. They have mowed the meadow below the garden, part of the dry ground.

June 13. Started and finished the skirt of my new dress, Mother helped me cut it out and make it, a plain skirt with a frill of the bordering, Louie is making the blouse for me, sailor fashion, with a vest of old lace. Harry took Jock over to Ringwood and brought back the chestnut mare. Uncle has not paid him and he did not enjoy himself at all! Mrs. Farrance is better but Mrs. Epps is nursing her mother and is really not well enough to do it. Letter from Auntie Ria and Mr. Deacon and the Bible Union. Went out with the gun, no chances.

June 14. Mr. and Mrs. Cole came for the day; Harry met them in the morning and drove them down to the bus at night. It is three years since they came last to see us and are living at West End [Southampton]. We had tea out of doors. We sent Miss Bingham a box of flowers and each wrote to her to thank her for our presents. Mr. and Mrs. Venvell and Mr. Egerton came up in the evening; they close at 5.00 now on Wednesday. Mr. V. and I went round with the gun, rode Joey bare backed and played cricket. Mr. Egerton tried to get a shot but we all failed. I had a tiny ride, astride barebacked on Dad's chestnut mare in the field when they were showing her to Mr. and Mrs. Coles. They came partly to see her but Mr. Cole would not give Dad's price. Dick let Joey slip and took the skin off his knee. Trimmed my new hat, it looks very nice, with the white chiffon and speckled feathers. Mrs. Venvell brought me a little knitted work bag in brown string.

June 15. Mother had a letter from Mr. Seymour saying that anything that we want to send to Mr. Sampson must be sent before the 20th and also that funds are needed for pea meal and flour. We have all subscribed and made up to 25/6d. and hope to do more amongst friends tomorrow. I sent a card to Maude to tell her and Mother is writing to Mr. and Mrs. Mason to ask them to get us some tin plates to send out. At their last Xmas dinner they had no plates to give the children their dinner on. I have dressed one doll and partly dressed another. Louie finished my frock; it is so cool and pretty. Did some ironing, got up a white skirt. Dusted each of Miss May's rooms, we heard from her today that she is coming on Saturday and has enclosed a kind of bill of fare. Harry drove to Lyndhurst to get the American Organ [purchased on 9 June] and had Joe shod. The Philips are in great trouble, Charley, Mr. P's favourite son, is dying they think, he has congestion of the lung and was taken ill on Sunday night[63]. I am so sorry for them all.

---

[63] Charles Philips recovered from this illness.

June 16. Mr. Cheeseman came up to do the borders and brought his little boy and girl again; they are funny little mites. The boy Alfred won't be kissed, when Louie saw them she went to kiss them both, but Alfie quickly drew back! Mrs. Evans came in just before tea, Annie and I rode a little way with her, she was going to Minstead. Neddy Compton helped the boys mow and they've got all the dry ground grass down. Mrs. Hendy was out today in the Parks and has been for a drive, I am so very glad to hear that she is out of her room. Mr. Venvell is very bad with a gathering in his face.

June 17. Miss May has come and Miss French, she is such a stately, gracious lady, so handsome, with almost white hair. I rode down to Mr. Scamell's after tea to get my hymns for tomorrow morning. Willie was at home only for Sunday though. I gave Mrs. S. a ride on my bicycle much to the amusement of the onlookers. Saw Florrie [May], she will play in the evening. Mr. F. Short has gone to Cornwall, hence his absence. Old Mr. Short went to Southampton with Dad yesterday. Mr. Farmers came and bought the cow. It has been very hot today. Mr. Marchant said he was coming up today but of course he didn't come, I saw him tonight and Mrs. M. They gave me some lovely pinks and Amy gave me a piece of shrub, B – something *Globosia*[64], like tiny oranges the flower is and smells like honey.

[*June 18.*] Harry drove Miss May and me down to Emery Down; Miss M[ay] to Sunday Sch. and I, ditto and with playing the organ on my mind. However, it was not so bad after all. During the first hymn it was very asthmatical but got better afterwards. Actually, there were 3 of the choir present. Annie rode her bicycle both ways, also Willie. Charley Philips is better and going on nicely [see 15 June]. I played Miss May's accompanyments [*sic*] after tea for her on the new organ. It is a very nice toned one and the knee swells are so nice to use. I've never had anything to do with an American organ before. Kitty can't be found: Dad and H. and W. all went out after tea, thinking that she might be in a drain. They couldn't find her and got wet through almost – it came on to rain about 4.00 p.m. and rained till about 10.00 p.m., we need it! Miss French is very pleasant and nice, she came to tea with us. She is an Irish Lady, a friend of Mrs. Forbes.

June 19. Lovely morning after the rain, the roses smell beautifully. I had a nice letter from Maude telling me that poor little Rough is dead; he was poorly and Uncle sent him to the Vet's and he died there. Maude thinks it is so sad that there should be no one with him at the end! and they are all very sorry. He was such a sweet little dog and they all loved him so much. Mr. and Mrs. Hendy [? Fenely] and three friends called to see Grandpa. Miss May and Miss French and Louie have gone out for lunch and tea picnics today. Miss May has given us some comforters for Mr. Sampson that she has had crotchetted [*sic*] and we have done up the parcel; 30/- for pea meal, 6 dolls and some books and 6 wraps and Dickie and I drove the chestnut mare down to Post. She went very well but does not always pass well, she wants waking up a little, and she got it!! It is the first time that I've driven my lady. Louie commenced driving by taking charge of Joe whilst Miss May and Miss F. had lunch. Harry took Poppet and Kitty across to Seymours. Heavy rain again this evening.

June 20. Showery day. Miss May and Miss French drove to Ocknell Pond this morning and the carriage came at 1.30 and Miss May saw her off at Brockenhurst and brought Miss Morris, the E[mery] Down Sch Mistress up to tea. She is so shy and quiet. The coachman waited and took her back in the carriage. Tom Lane [aged 19 years] came down for a bit for Harry and to see Miss May. He has changed his mind and is going to Ashford, not London. Mr. Forbes is getting him in to some carriage works there. Harry went to Ings's with Jenny. Began a letter to Maude.

June 21. I drove Miss May through Rinefields [*sic*] to Brockenhurst St[ation]. this morning. I've not been in that Inclosure since I was about 8 or 10 years old and went with Mr. and Mrs. Forbes and Harry, quite in my young days. I called at Amy's coming back, she wanted me to go to a C. E. Picnic and Meeting on Balmer Green, Brockenhurst, with her this afternoon, but is impossible. Made inquiries about Miss French's lost sable collar. Letters from Mrs. Coles and White and Missionary Leaves receipt for the £1.10s. we sent. Picked 9lb. of green gooseberries and preserved them. Miss May has gone to London for a day or two, she

---

[64] Most probably, *Buddleia globosa*

returns on Friday evening with Miss E. Briggs. Mrs. Venvell is very poorly, run down with a bad cold. Made a resolution not to shoot rabbits!

June 22. Dr. White[65] called this morning to see Grandpa and brought his two little girls with him. They are such nice little ders; I took them round the yard. Helped Dick rake up into rows and pook(?) the hay in the big meadow whilst the others carted the dry ground hay. It came on to rain just after Mother and Annie and Lou had brought tea down into the field. We finished indoors, whilst in the field, however, Rev. and Mrs. and Miss Maturin came to see Grandpa, they had tea in the veranda and enjoyed themselves they said. Rev. Maturin is such a funny old gentleman, he talks so abruptly. The rain did not come to much; it is very close. Louie and I packed Auntie Annie some flowers.

June 23. Got up at 5.00 and got my work done and went into Southampton. We meant to start at 6.00 but got off at 7.00. Saw Auntie and Uncle James, he is very poorly indeed and weak. Got in to Hendy's fairly early, Lizzie and I went shopping in the morning, had dinner there, Dada too, and we started directly afterwards. Lizzie came out as far as Chandlers with us and Dad saw someone pass that they knew and she rode home with him. Mrs. Venvell is still very poorly. I have got rather a headache. We got home at 5.30 after having tea at Mr. and Mrs. Venvell's. Carted what hay we have about. Mrs. Taylor died last Friday[66] and is buried, we saw Dick. Miss May and Miss Briggs came late, at 10.00 p. m.

June 24. Rode down to get my hymns, had tea with Mrs. Evans and helped her plant out some plants. It is Thursday now and I'm writing up as each evening I've been either too tired or to[o] busy to write. Sunday. Alf came out and led the singing, it was a great help – got on better. I had the two little Squire boys in the gallery and talked to them. Old Emma was very ill, we called in but didn't see her; she died in the evening I think.

[There are no diary entries for the period 25 to 28 June, inclusive. The entries for 29 and 30 June are written on the back inside cover of the exercise book.]

June 29ᵗʰ. I must miss out those few days. We have been to the Hon. A. Herbert's tea[66] and I've got a good headache. Alf came out in time to go with us, Dad and Dick and I drove over and Harry and the rest. Murray Petty came in to dinner. Two ladies, friends of Mr. Duckworth's, called to see Grandpa and get refreshments, they were cycling. We had lots of visitors yesterday. Miss Eyre and her lady companion to tea and to see Grandpa. Mr. and Mrs. Jeffreys and two friends to tea and afterwards Lizzie and Mrs. and Miss Child and Mrs. Pechil. Miss C. had a puncture and Annie and Lizzie mended it for her. I drove down with Miss May and Miss Briggs to the Station, there were 100s of people there keeping up Coronation Day[68].

June 30ᵗʰ. Mother went to Southampton. It has been a lovely morning, but it came on to rain at about 4 o'clock and it is still raining steadily. I have been out flower gathering for the vases. Mother had a telegram from Miss May, she is not coming tonight. Mrs. Bateman brought two friends up, Mrs Macauley[69] and her daughter, to see Grandpa. She did not stay to tea but had milk and cake. They drove up in a carriage and pair. Mr. Richard Light is dying and his wife is ill too and Uncle James is still very weak. We hear of so many deaths and yet we are spared ourselves. Mr. Short has got a cold. Miss Briggs has sent me a basket of chocolates and a nice little note addressed to the "Deputy Organist" and spelling my name "Be" and a note for Annie and 2/6 to get a pr of gloves with, in any colour she likes.

[Diary continued in the second notebook.]

[65] Dr. Barrington White (see biographical notes).

[66] Mrs Elizabeth Taylor, died on 16 June, aged 55. She was interred on the 18 June in Copythorne churchyard.

[67] The teas arranged by the Hon. Auberon Herbert and his daughter, Nan, were renowned far and wide. They were held at their Burley residence and were known as 'The Old House Teas' which could be enjoyed 'As Long as the Tea-Pot Lasts'. (see Hardcastle, F., *Records of Burley* (1987), p. 126.)

[68] Commemorating and celebrating the coronation of Queen Victoria, 27 June 1838.

[69] Mrs Macauley is likely to be Mrs. Macleay who lived at Glasshayes, Lyndhurst. Her husband, Col. Alexander Macleay (d.1907) is commemorated on an inscription in Lyndhurst church. The diarist may have misheard or misremembered the name.

July 1. 99. Saturday. Miss May and Miss Laura Taylor came at lunch time, it has been a very wet day, such heavy showers. Dada drove over to the Lights to see Mr R Light and he was with him half an hour before he died; he was unconscious when Dad was there. Harry and Willie drove to Hill Top, Beaulieu to the Hendy's workmen's outing. None of the family were there and the boys expected to meet Alf but he was not there. Maude has sent me a lovely painted plaque, her own work, a spray of Virginia Creeper, she has done it beautifully. Sent off P.O. for Alice's birthday gift.

July 2. Another showery day; we got to Chapel in a fine part of the day but had a shower or two coming home. Will rode my machine home; I did not bicycle at all. Miss May rode to early service. It is Communion Sunday – we are going to have a weekly Communion now.

July 3. Wrote a hurried note to Alice and sent her a box of flowers for tomorrow. Had a letter from Maude. Miss May brought it and told me that she was afraid she had lost it and Ellen found it in her pocket so it was all the sweeter for delay! Miss May and Miss Taylor drove down to tea at the Vicarage [Emery Down]. Harry went down with the trucks. N.B. no washing sent. More showers again and a fire is quite pleasant, it's not at all July weather. Miss May is making a list of all the books with Miss T's help. Read the story of *Henry Clark* to Grandpa this evening. Painted the stair in preparation for the new carpet.

July 4. Rather hotter today, no rain. One of the telegraph boys came up with the letters today. Herbert has left. Miss May and Miss Taylor drove to Lyndhurst after tea. Made meringues, in very short notice, they turned out well but the cream would *not* whip. Mr., Miss and Mr. (Junr) Molyneux, and Mrs. M's brother, came this afternoon, Dr. Palmer, who is one of the most famous commentators on the Bible at the present day. Alice's birthday.

July 5. Very hot day. Miss May and Miss Taylor went out for a picnic lunch, in for tea. Mrs Evans and Miss Otten cycled up this evening and stayed a little while. Alf came out later on the motor tricycle, after their choir outing. Wrote to Eveline. Had a disappointment; I was to go on Harry's mare for the cows, the first time and Harry came with the cows just as I'd got the mare saddled and I had to do without my ride.

July 6. Miss May and Miss Taylor and Louie have gone to London; Lou bound for Tunbridge Wells and Miss May and Miss T. for Keswick. I have got Pumpkin to care for. We went for a walk this evening and found some white heather. They got in Mills' mare this morning, we all helped. Harry saw her as he was coming home from the St[ation when] he took the luggage down. Alf went at about 9 o'clock. Mother and I painted the back kitchen and Annie cleaned the paint and Mother did pieces of whitewashing.

July 7. I rode for the cows on Harry's young mare, she is a dear. I found them near Halfpenny Green. Pumpkin had a severe shock and bolted. He has been out all day and has not turned up yet, old wretch! Dickie rode the chestnut mare to Southampton. Mr. Coles has bought her after all. Sent Alice and Maude some white heath[er] and roses. Mr. Stag drove up the Vicar of Eling's wife and child and two ladies and wanted us to get them tea; we did, to oblige him. They were very pleasant and charmed with the place. Mrs. Hendy is very poorly. Picked some raspberries and helped [unclear three-lettered word] some of the hay after tea and went up to Lanes about Pumpkin.

July 8. Pumpkin did not come back but Mother went out and found him up at the top with three dry mare's ribs in his mouth from which I suppose he proudly imagined he was gaining nourishment!! He had 9 "hard hits" and has been chained up all day outside. I drove to meet Auntie and Uncle at the bus this afternoon. The buses were late, saw Fred Short Esqr. he was just starting to come up and photograph Grandpa, he has taken him in several positions. We had some music. Had a nice letter from Alice, she is delighted with her Veeder. It has been intensely hot.

July 9. Alf joined us at Chapel and Dick rode his bicycle home and he came in the trap. Annie bicycled down and stayed to Communion with Brownie who is staying with Mrs. Jeanes. Willie and Harry went to bed and rested. We had a pleasant walk in the evening. Mrs. Hendy is not any better or worse.

July 10. We have had a rushing day, first part getting the washing done. Mr. Freeman came up and looked at the pump, the pipe is cracked and it will be a 2 days' job. I rode for the cows on Harry's mare, went round to the Saw Bench and found them at last lying down on the Green. Mr. and Mrs. Jeanes and Mrs. Scamell and Brownie came up to tea and then Mrs. Evans and her brother Stanley came and, whilst we were all at tea, Mr. Browning came, and Mr. and Mrs. Wright and their little boy and a friend, Miss Lena. They had tea when we had done. I have been writing in the dark, consequently - !! Have picked some merrys[70]. [The following words struck through.] Have had lovely ride

July 11. Very hot day, we are haymaking and they find it very hot in the fields. Mother, Auntie and I drove down to Lyndhurst with Joey after tea, called at Mrs. Scamell's and took the books back, then went on to Mrs. Payne's. She was so busy and they didn't see much of her. Mr. S. has lent three beautiful books. Had a card from Lil [probably Liz.] to ask me to come and saying that they can't get away as Mr. Hendy is away. I replied. Alf wrote to Dad about a place near Winchester for sale.

Rev Tom Webb Scamell at the door of Lyndhurst Baptist Church. Photograph probably by Fredrick Golden Short

July 12. Our Chapel Anniversary and General Tea fight. Annie and I rode down; I went first and took some flowers and buttonholes for a select few! There were very few people there. The speakers were Revs Collins, Egerton, Brooker, Joy and Payne, our old minister, and Rev. Scamell with his Report. Lillie and Florrie [May] rode our bicycles about, enjoyed ourselves quietly. I rode for the cows this morning and found them in Rush Moors.

July 13. The children's tea and Romps were on today. I drove Mother and Auntie down and we came home before 7 o'clock to my great disgust for I was just in a game of cricket on Mr. Bowden-Smith's side, his first pick! The other side were in first and I had to go before we had our innings. I was mad! I rode for the cows again and found them quite close on Bratley Green. I shot a thrush and a sparrow this morning. Dada told me to shoot at the birds in the cherries and I did and happened to kill!

July 14. Dad got back from Southampton early, before 6.00. Mrs. Hendy is no worse. It has been raining today, a fine rain that began before 7.00 and kept on until *after* 11.00, but cleared up in the afternoon. Auntie and I picked some red currants and raspberries. They got on to the hay directly after tea and I walked for the cows to Bratley Green and caught Poppet and rode her home. A letter came for us today which was meant for Mrs. Lane, a party from Parkstone Easter – something was the name of the house. Auntie and I took it up to her and she knew about it.

July 15. We had plenty of visitors here today. To begin with, two men called asking for lemonade, they came twice. Then Miss Eliott of the Bourne School came and asked if she and seven of her girls might have their lunch here, and they did. They were very nice young ladies. They have cycling runs on Saturdays, etc., and they were all riding today. Miss and Mrs. Clough came too and put up their horses here, 3 ladies and 1 gentleman on horseback. Miss Florence Clough and a friend came in and asked us to give her sisters a message. Mr. and Mrs. Herbert Goss and another lady and gentleman came soon after tea and begged that we would get them tea. Mr. Goss has been here before and they know a lot of Mother's friends in Surbiton, so we did. I rode for the cows, found them on Halfpenny Green and saw 3 lovely fallow deer in Bushy Bratley, two splendid bucks. Made jam, raspberry and red currant, 11lbs of fruit. I think that we've had enough visitors for one day! They have got nearly all the hay up.

---

[70] Fruit of the gean or wild cherry

July 16. Harry drove Auntie to Chapel with his mare. Mother and I stayed to Communion, there were very few there, only 10. I began reading *Little Men*[71] to Dickie, we sat in the orchard. We all had a lovely walk up to Bushy Bratley.

July 17. Annie went in to Southampton, she rode her bicycle down to Lyndhurst and went in by train and had a tooth out. She is going to have a new set at the bottom. Mrs. Mason and Ernie have come back with her, they have all bicycled, Ernie, all the way. It has been very hot today. I gathered 12lbs of gooseberrys [sic] and preserved them. It was hot work. I shot two birds in the cherries. We have had a game of cricket this evening. I have got a postcard from Miss May, she is coming on Saturday and bringing a young lady to stay with her for charity; she needs a change and is poor. They have got all the hay in. Harry took Merry and Joey to be shod and he is bringing back the trap from Austin's on approval. He got home at 11.00 – he was so hindered.

July 18. Mrs. Mason and Ernie helped me pick some blackcurrants; we gathered 13lbs. I preserved them with 3lbs of bl[ac]k merrys. Uncle and Harry and Will drove Harry's mare to Whiteparish and Dean and they went to Salisbury and got home at about 9 o'clock after having spent a very pleasant day. Auntie and Mrs. Mason and I walked to meet them and we saw a bird asleep on a briar and had a big discussion as to what it was and they can't tell us and have suggested all they can think of from a sparrow to a partridge! I started for the cows on Jesse, but saw Dick and Ernie coming with them. Ernie has got a bilious attack and is rather queer. He shot a thrush today. Jim Deacon has sent us some of his wedding cake, he was married on Dad's and Mother's wedding day. Another very hot day. We are going to Beaulieu tomorrow for the day.

July 19. Dad and Mother and Auntie and Uncle and Dick and I drove to Beaulieu. We went through Rinefields [sic] and Mark Ash, a long way round. We had lunch near Lady Cross and Jesse threw half a shoe soon after and we had him shod at Beaulieu. We went over the Abbey and Church and generally admired the place and enjoyed it very much. We had tea at a very nice little place. We got home at 6 o'clock and picked the raspberrys [sic] and a lot of bl[ac]k currants. It was very hot even driving and the perspiration dripped off him. Miss Clough came and had tea here. I have got a headache to conclude with! Harry has gone to Poulner with Poppet and Kitty. I went for the cows on Merry this morning.

July 20. Harry and Will started for Whiteparish before breakfast and brought the mares home, they are not any better for the keep. I rode Jesse for the cows and got well shook up and felt very queer and laid down for most of the morning. It was chronic for a bit! However, I'm alright now. I drove Annie and Mother to Mr. William Davis's, we had tea there and saw their separator [sic][72] at work and all their cattle, they are a fine lot. Two of the girls had gone to Tunbridge Wells today and only two were at home. Had a letter from Maude, she and Alice are going to N. Devon with Lou and Allan – I am dismalapointed[73] but I hope to get there yet. I shall write tonight.

July 21. Auntie and Uncle [Croxford] have gone home today. I drove them to the bus with Joey. We are sorry they have gone but Uncle has to be at the [British] Museum on Monday, and Saturday is such a bad day for travelling – they like to be quieter. Dad has a postcard from Miss May, she is not coming until Monday and bringing two young ladies with her, she is at Ware. Mrs. Mason went home this evening; I rode to Emery Down with her and found a parcel of books he had dropped, from Mrs Evans books returned and some *Girls Own* for us to read and a note for me. A thunderstorm has come on and the lightening [sic] and thunder are pretty stiff and it's so hot. Poor Mrs. Hendy is very poorly, the heat I expect. I sent a letter to Maude today and I *do* hope they'll come. It'll be hard lines if they don't.

July 22. The thunder did not come to much last night and the heat has been burning today. We had a letter from Auntie Annie – they got home alright and Jack welcomed them ['enthusiastically' struck through] with joy! Auntie wrote at 9.30 p.m. and we got it the next morning. Auntie Rye has written and Miss May, she [is] coming on Monday with Miss Starling and the fresh girl. She has a lovely voice, Miss May says and

---

[71] *Little Men* by Louisa May Alcott (1832-88)
[72] A device to separate cream from milk (possibly an Alfa-Laval Separator).
[73] A made up word from dismal and disappointed.

Miss S. plays beautifully so perhaps we shall have some nice music. Dad and Harry and Will have been hoeing mangel all day. Mother has made some black currant jam.

July 23. Ernie [Mason] and Dick and I rode to Chapel, I got down in time to play the hymn at S[unday] School. It was very thundery but did not come to rain. Fred Short has sent us four of Grandpa's photos, one of each position, they are splendid. We met a Mr. James Reilly coming home from Chapel: he had lost his dog and we promised to call at Mr. Lane's and ask them to look out for it, but we met the dog on the road, trotting straight for home. The back tyre cover of Ernie's steed began to burst out by the valve, so we let the air out and I bound it up and it bore him home.

July 24. It is more windy today. We have had a busy time with washing and preparing for Miss May. She has not come yet and it is nearly 10 o'clock! Harry and Dada have been after Whitefoot, they had a splendid run and Harry put the saddle on Whitefoot in the Forest and went after someone's heifer, the horses went splendidly. Miss May and Miss Beatrice Dunn and Miss B. Starling came just after 10.00. It was 12 o'clock before we got to bed.

Old Henry Tame aged 103 years. Photographed in 1899 by Fredrick Golden Short

July 25. I had a letter from Mrs Evans this morning asking Annie and I to go to Lymington with them tomorrow but it is impossible so I rode down as far as her house with Ernie. He has gone home today, but she was out for a ride. I saw old Mr. Short and walked up the Street with him and had a chat with Miss Short. When I got home I found Mr. and Mrs. W. Davies and their daughter Nellie. They stayed to supper and we walked round in the dark. She is such a nice girl. They brought some lovely roses and other flowers. Mrs. Scamell and her Mother came up in a donkey cart, with a boy to "stoke-up". They got up just before tea and went soon after. Mrs. S. brought up two dolls for Miss May to see. It was 12 again before we got to bed. Dad caught Miss May smoking and was pained and surprised!

July 26. Miss May, Miss Starling and Miss Dunn have each dressed a doll for the Emery Down Treat, Ellen has finished them off. Sydney Hughes came up for the day with them and they washed Pumpkin and went for a picnic in the afternoon.

July 27. Tulip has two dear little bull calves. She is the first cow that we have that's had twins. They brought them in the handcart, their pram! Miss May has gone to the Treat with her two friends. They enjoyed it but Miss May was very tired. I went for the cows on Jesse and had a long ride but couldn't find them. I left home at a little after 5.00 and got in at 8.45. I have not had such a ride on my side saddle for a long time, the ground is very hard for riding. The sunset was glorious, lovely colours. I saw an old woman on the road walking to Stoney Cross, tramping, she was quite old and very pitiful to look at and we had a chat, I asked her home to have

A new calf in a hand cart with the mother cow following. Beatrice writes, 'They brought them in the handcart, their pram' (27 July)

some tea but she preferred to keep on. She says she does bits of needlework for people as her eyes are so good and she has walked from Scotland, started late last Autumn and has braved the storms. She said she wanted to walk along the coast and get the 'breezes'. She keeps out of towns as she doesn't like to hear the 'scoffers'. She had no friend but God and the spiritual life around her and seemed quite content so far.

July 28. Fred Short came up in the evening to be ready to take the photos of Miss May and Pumpkin tomorrow. He's brought his rifle. Heard that Lizzie is driving the motor alone, with Cissie. I expect she's the first lady driver in Southampton! Miss May and Miss Starling and Miss Dunn each played to Mr. Frederick. I played Miss May's accompaniments.

July 29. Mr. S[hort] was up early with his rifle. I had a few shots with it at a tin can. I only hit once in 5 or 6 shots. Fred has taken a lot of photos of them about the place and Pumpkin and went home directly after tea. The 3 ladies have driven to Lyndhurst tonight.

July 30. I drove Miss S. and Miss Dunn down [to Chapel] with one trap and Joe; Miss May bicycled and Will rode her Machine back. Mother and he and I stayed behind to Communion. I have begun reading the tale in the *Sunday at H* this evening – George came last Friday for his holiday.

Aug. 1. Miss May fetched Mrs. Hughes and S[ydney] H[ughes] up for the day, they had all three meals outside and made a lot of extra work. Got flowers and did the vases. Fred tried to take a photo of the twins on Saturday but they would not keep still a second. Mrs. H. and her boy bicycled home after dinner.

July 31. It is very hot indeed now, they've finished harvesting ['yesterday' struck through]. Harry went out with Mr. C. Tanner ['yesterday' struck through] colt hunting ['yesterday' struck through] on Merry, all day – they only got one colt. My notes are behind hand and I am writing up a week later than the actual time, practise for memory. I've muddled the days. Monday Miss May took S. Hughes and the Misses S[tarling] and D[unn] to Bournemouth for the day. I rode to Lyndhurst and found Mrs. Marshall has been very ill and is now. I saw her, but she is so weak. Miss Dunn keeps on getting bitten and her face swells very much, each eye is bad. And ['on Sat.' struck through] it stopped them going to Winchester one day.

Aug. 2. Wednes. Miss Starling went and Pumpkin, Miss May and Miss D[unn] drove her to the St[ation] and had tea out and took Pumpkin to Colonel Austin. He is going to keep him when she is away for her [sentence unfinished.]

[No entry for 3 August.]

Aug. 4. About 6 o'clock Pumpkin appeared in Louie's room; he had come back, poor doggie. He knows more than he's credited for I think! Miss May has gone, and Miss Dunn. Miss May is off to Germany tonight for ten days, for Frau Keever's birthday and to fetch Fraulien over. I've sent Frau K. a card and written on it 'Hier ist ein Blünchen für Sie' on it – my old sentence to make her laugh! Lou has gone to Felixstowe for the time. Pumpkin is taken back to Colonel Austin's. I rode to Lyndhurst after tea to see Mrs. Marshall chiefly. I stayed with her about ½ an hour, Mrs. Scamell and Jeanes came whilst I was there – Mr. Jeanes says he meets me everywhere he goes! Saw Mrs.

Lyndhurst as the Tames knew it. The Short family had their premises in the shop on the right, just beyond the cart.
Photograph by John Golden Short

Stairs, she wants me to go over on Monday. Johnnie Lane came down to borrow a bicycle pump to pump up a hired bicycle with. Three ladies came who are staying at Burley and had lost themselves, Dad took them through Oakly [sic]. [Inserted vertically in the margin: 'Harry went over to Woodfords.']

Aug. 5. It is so hot and oppressive, we are hoping for rain. They have been colt hunting today, got in Farmer's young mare and Mr. Goff's colt which Harry has bought for the Fair next week. I have made two ties and done other needlework and partly written up this tonight. Mother had a letter from Aunt Louie and Aunt Pollie and a p.c. from Fred Short; he thinks he has left his camp stool.

Aug. 6. [First two lines of this entry in pencil.] Annie and I rode our bicycles to Chapel. Alf met us there and came on. Mr. John Short was at Chapel. Mr. Barton came just as we had got tea outside, he wrote to Annie on Saturday saying that he was coming down and would like to come up on Monday for a few hours, to see Grandpa, so we were both pleased and surprised to see him. He stayed the night and went out with Dad for the cows.

Aug. 7. *Bank Holiday.* It has been a rather dull day, rain in the morning and afternoon. Mr. Frampton and a party, and a Mr. Broomfield and party called to see Grandpa. Dick and I bicycled over to Mr. and Mrs. Stairs' picnic, it was very nice and we had a good game of cricket. Alf brought Mr. and Mrs. Pechil out in the motor to the picnic. Harry and Will and Georgie drove Mr. Barton round Rufus Stone and to the "Trusty Servant"[74] from where he walked into Lyndhurst. They got to Mrs. Stairs at about 7.30. We stayed a little time longer and talked to Mrs. and Miss Dunning and then came home, got here about 9.30. The roads are awfully loose and stiff. Dad went to Thorney Hill and presided at the Meeting there. Mr. Woodford came this morning and the boys helped him in with the colt Harry has bought from him for the Fair.

Aug. 8. Tobe Gailor came over early and they started for the mare of Mill's they've bought and hunted for so much and got her at Hinchesly [*sic*] and brought her home; they got home at about 8.30. I helped Dick milk etc., and got a ride in the dark. The colts had got in to the meadows and I turned them out. Poppet slipped me and went down to the lower meadow and when I got her I jumped on her and had a fine gallop up. I've not enjoyed ['had' interlined above] any bareback riding for a long time till tonight. I drove Mother to Lyndhurst to Mrs. Payne's. We saw Mrs. Marshall – she was in the garden and is much better out of the Doctor's hands now! Had a letter from Miss Dunn telling me of her safe arrival at Barnes and missing the "Farm". Annie heard from Lou – they missed their trains.

Aug. 9. Lyndhurst Fair today. Harry took the old liver coloured mare and her colt and the two colts ['Goff's and Woodford's' interlined above] and Farmer's young mare. They got very small prizes for 4, £1.10s. for Farmer's mare and brought back Woodford's colt and they have printed it. I rode Merry for the cows – found them at "Stinking Hedges". All the boys went to the fair. Dick bought me some pears and burnt almonds. Have had a good practise at pieces this evening and done a lot of machining for Mother.

Aug. 10. It has been a lovely day. I drove Mother over to see Mrs. Retford, but we did not stay as the Hon. A. Herbert was there and everyone else was away. She was so very busy, we just saw her and drove home. The drive was lovely and the heather down their road is lovely. Harry and Georgie went to Fritham to hunt for the heifer and couldn't find her. Frank Lane came down to ask about Miss May's trap for Mr. Pink. Wrote a line to Aggie.

Aug. 11. Annie went into Southampton to have 2 teeth out etc., it was a nasty job. Poor Mrs. Hendy doesn't seem to get any better. Uncle James is going to work now, their servant told Dad. The boys are potatoe [*sic*] digging. Began a letter to Eveline at last.

Aug. 12. Have just finished Eveline's letter. She came up to Winsor on Wednesday, and Percy. I expect her Father and Mother come up today. Mrs. Austin has been here and brought Pumpkin back; he fights with her dog so that she thought it best to fetch him back. I have been out on Joey for the cows, the first ride I've had on him. He goes well – it's a job to hold him coming home. Have had letters from Aunties Polly and Ria and from Aggie – she was so pleased with her flowers and note.

Aug. 13. Got down to Chapel early to play at S[unday] School and the harmonium was in the Chapel so I played the first tune there and they put the Sch Room door open to hear. Fred asked me to play the last hymn for him as he wanted to go somewhere. We had the harmonium downstairs and I sat with the "Choir". I got on all right with the hymn. Willie didn't know that I played!! Arthur Taylor and Miss Evemy came just as we'd finished tea, they meant to drive through the Inclosures but the gates are all locked so they had some tea and spent the time with us and we went out for a walk. I rode to Chapel alone.

---

[74] A public house in Minstead (it is still there).

Aug. 14. Dick and I rode the bicycles in to Southampton and had them seen to; my frame was wrenched out and the back forks. Annie's had 3 balls broken. The wind was against us going in and we got tired so we came out by train and Alf came with us. He was very kind and gave us a ride in a motor down the town. Mary and D. and I went to Hythe on the boat in the afternoon. Enjoyed our day very much though we are very tired.

Aug. 15. Lizzie is going to Boscombe today. George and I drove to Lyndhurst in the evening. It is so very hot, it makes one feel like lying down all day. Alf went early, at 6. Mrs. Scamell and her niece and Mrs. Morant and a friend drove up to see Grandpa, we met them coming up. Tobe came yesterday and they went to the Mills' and he was not generous at all. They rode out and looked for the heifers this afternoon. Mother heard from Miss May, she and Fraulien come tomorrow and Mr. F[orbes] this week too, for her birthday. Am very tired tonight.

Aug. 16. The rain has not come yet, we do need it so. Mr. Joe Stride's crippled daughter has just come with Mr. ['George' struck through] Emery to see Grandpa, she was such a bright child Mother says and kept house for her Father. She was alright till she took a chill after an illness and it left her crippled, poor child. I went out before breakfast and got berries and flowers for the vases and did them – they took such a time. Mr. Luckham has just called to see Grandpa: he has come out with a party and just called. Miss Stride and her Uncle stayed to tea. Miss May and Fraulien and Louie have come. Fraulien seems quite pleased to be here again – it is nice to have her here again. Miss May has brought some new songs, we tried them over after dinner. A gentleman and little boy asked Fraulien the way to Burley when she was out; she couldn't tell them so they came down. They are going to Holmsey [*sic*] and we directed them and gave them some milk and cake. Miss May has brought me a foot-pump, for looking after Pumpkin.

Aug. 17. Miss May and Fraulien rested all the morning and drove to Lyndhurst in the evening. Mrs. W Payne and Mr. and Mrs. Jenkins (her niece and *her* husband). They had early tea and left at 3.30 and Mrs. Jenkins left her sunshade. I rode down after tea and took it. Fraulien has brought us each a present – Annie, Lou and I brooches, the boys, tie pins, Mother a card tray and Dad an ornamental glass. My brooch is so pretty, a wee miniature in filligree setting. The rivet was out of the pin so I took it to Mr May[75] and he repaired it for me. It was very kind of him indeed; I called at their house and spent a short time with the girls.

Aug. 18. Harry went in with Dad to be measured for a suit. Sydney Hughes came up for the day with Miss May. He walked back and left the "Singer" bicycle. Pumpkin had another narrow escape – Ben and Spring both embracing him!

Aug. 19. Mother had a letter from Aunt Louie saying that Arthur was coming today. He got here at 5.00 p.m. – he was 6 hours riding the 92 miles, a good pace to keep up! We gave Miss May her presents today instead of tomorrow as she is going to early Church. I dressed Pumpkin up for tea and took him to her. We have given her a letter scale. She made a lovely cake today and then we took it out before it was done and it burst and was liquid inside, it is such a disappointment for her. Fraulien has given her a tea set, chinese china. I rode to Emery Down in the evening, the air was full of thunder flies and it was so hot.

Aug. 20. All drove to Chapel. It is Miss May's birthday. She and Fraulien went to Chapel with Harry and I played for Fred as he had some friends and wanted to spend his time with them. Sophie Stansbridge[76] was baptised this evening. Miss May and I stayed to supper with the Hughes and walked back. Harry was very queer in Chapel, almost fainted, but he got out in time and sat down.

Aug. 21. Harry is not much better today. Miss May drove to Brockenhurst St[ation] to meet her Father and Mr. Fleet, drove home with Joey and Miss May and Sydney Hughes came in the carriage and they all had a picnic coming home. Wrote a note to Eveline. Arthur rode to Lyndhurst and came back in 9 minutes.

---

[75] Edward May of the High Street, Lyndhurst, (next to Short's the chemist) the watch maker who replaced the rivet.
[76] She was then aged 19 years.

Aug. 22. No letter from Maude again. I went out with Mr. Forbes and Miss May for a drive to Ocknell Pond. It was very lovely and the evening was delightful.

Aug. 23. Uncle and Auntie Farrance and Mr Pearse and Mrs Epps and her nephew came over this afternoon to tea and stayed till 7.0. They were all very well. Tobe Gailor came over this morning about a mare for sale belonging to Mr Mills's son. Harry and George and he drove to Mills and bought the mare. Arthur and Dick drove Whitefoot to the St[ation] for Arthur's bag. Had a letter from Mary Hendy, she can't come on Friday as Lil [*sic*, Liz] is staying at Boscombe longer but wants me to go in – but I can't. Mr. Forbes, Miss May and Mr. Fleet went for a drive in the evening.

August 24. [the verse lines in Arthur Webb's hand.]

> Nice day.
>
> Went to Winsor.
>
> Sung a song.
>
> Went down a treat.
>
> Une to me.
>
> Nothing unusual.
>
> [Four lines heavily obliterated in ink.]
>
> Not used to it.
>
> [Single line heavily obliterated.]
>
> Now we shan't be long.
>
> Thine for ever Pimpy. Arthur Webb, grand composer!

I rode to Winsor in the afternoon and Arthur came a little later as he was out with Harry when I started. It was very hot and the wind was against me going. They were all very nice to me and I was so glad to see them and we spent a very pleasant evening there and rode home between 8 and 9 without lighting. Pumpkin is bad and being fed with brandy.

[No entries recorded from 25 to 31 August, inclusive.]

Sept. 1. It is some time since I wrote my diary and I have a lot of write up. Auntie and Jimmie came last Saturday and are staying till Monday. I drove Auntie and Mother to Ringwood yesterday afternoon to see Auntie and Uncle. Auntie had heard of the death of her eldest sister and was of course rather upset. Mrs. Epps and Mr. Pearse and I had two games of croquet before tea and looked at the flowers. The double begonias were a dream, so very lovely.

Sept. 2. Henry came over on his bicycle. Mr. Sydney May came up with Arthur this morning and stayed the day. It was showery this evening.

Sept. 3. Played at Chapel morning and evening and rode my machine each time. Dick went with me in the evening, we were both very tired. I had to choose all the hymns and tunes today.

Sept. 4. Auntie and Jim went this morning, Auntie would go, we are very sorry to lose them. Jim has given me a photo of dear little Rough (or Podgernice!) [See 19 June.] They went out to look for Joey who has gone off with some wild mares and they can't get him. Henry went too this morning. Gave Mary her first bicycle lesson, one tumble and bruise!

Sept. 5. Rode to Lyndhurst in the evening. Picked 6½ lbs of blackberries and 9 lbs of Christian Plums. Miss Wilkinson and Mrs. Forman have sent me a very pretty scarf. They got old Joe in.

Sept. 6. We had a heavy thunderstorm all the morning, a splendid rain. Fine and hot all the rest of the day. George went blackberrying, took out 2 half gallon baskets and picked about 1½ lbs of berrys [sic], not quite, he's going to make it up tomorrow! Wonder if it's true! Gave Mary a lesson again, she can nearly go alone. Had a P.C. from Alf saying that the wheel shall be sent and that he's coming on Saturday with Mr. and Mrs. Mason if possible and if the "Hotel" is not full. I rode down and got the wheel from Mr. Venvell's – he brought it and strapped it on my back for me and I carried it home so. It's made my back ache, tho'! Harry, Will and Arthur went out on horseback for the heifers, hunting for them, but can't find them. Arthur rode to Lyndhurst this morning.

Sept. 7. Went out blackberrying this morning, with George and Mary – we got a nice lot. We have had another heavy thunderstorm. At Cadnam they have not had any rain to speak of today and we've been nearly flooded. Mary and I drove over and took back Mr. and Mrs. Davis's basket, they were milking and I had a chat with them each in the cow pens and saw the other two girls, Rose and the other elder girls. We didn't stay long; Mrs D. gave us some pears. We met Sir W[illiam] Harcourt twice on our way, out driving. It is 10.0 and Miss May hasn't come yet. Miss May and Fraulien and Louie got in after 11.0. They missed their train at Southampton and had to wait an hour.

Sept. 8. George and Mary have gone home and Dick has been into town for the day. Mrs. Hendy is fairly well. Miss May and Fraulien drove to Lyndhurst. Mother had a letter from Mrs. Corke, her son Neville is coming tomorrow. A lady and gentleman called wanting lodgings.

Sep. 9. Master Neville Corke came this morning. Dickie went to meet him and missed him so he went on the Ringwood road and couldn't find the place and came in up the garden when he got here. We then went to meet Dick to tell him. Lou and I drove to Lyndhurst with Whitefoot, the first time that I've driven her. She went well, all except the start, we met Alf and Mrs. Mason and Alfie in the motor and Mr. Mason on his bicycle – they have come for Sunday. Willy and Arthur rode to Bournemouth on their bicycles for the day.

[There are no entries from the 10 September to the 23 November, inclusive. The final entry is written entirely in pencil.]

Nov. 24. My diary has not been kept, to say the least, regularly! And a sudden inspiration has made me write tonight. I can't write it all up unless I take about a month! Mr. Mason has come out tonight and Dad and the boy have been out with pigs all day. I have finished my new blue blouse. I got a letter from Maude this morning. Dick is wanting me to go to bed. I have just sent him off to bath – Saturday night![77] Operated on Grandpa's "pedal extremities"! I don't know how long my diary keeping will last (?).

[In fact it does not last for this is the final entry made by Beatrice.]

---

[77] Presumably, Saturday night is the weekly bath night. Bathing is not mentioned earlier in the diary.

Epilogue

As the diary entries cease rather abruptly on 9 September with just one half-hearted attempt to continue it again on 24 November, the reader is left wondering just what might have caused Beatrice Tame to give up recording daily life at Bolderwood Farm.

The diary was started in the early spring, when life on the farm is relatively quiet. Autumn is approaching as the diary ends, with harvest time and preparations for the winter. The whole family would have been busy with these extra tasks. Beatrice's grandfather was becoming frail and needed a great deal of nursing and attention. Her time would have been filled with all these extra demands. She had written so fully of the activities of the preceding months, with so much detail about all their visitors and the events on the farm throughout the season that it would have been daunting to continue the diary at that pace. She probably felt she would rather not write it at all than write it scantily or only sporadically.

But the bitter irony is that this account of the happy months of spring and summer at Bolderwood Farm was to be an account of the last happy period of life for the Tames of Bolderwood. Terrible events followed the end of the millennium for the Tame family that cast a dark shadow over the family which lasted well into the last century.

On 2 February 1900, Grandfather Tame came to the end of his life, having lived through three centuries and seeming almost immortal. This event, although hardly surprising, must have saddened all the Tames so much and life could never be quite the same again now that this formidable and loveable old man was no longer with them at Bolderwood.

But much worse was in store for the family in that year, 1900.

All four children loved horses, understood them, rode them, worked them and lived with them. They had grown up with horses and had no fear of them. The old working shire horses were intelligent, well behaved and well trained. They had their own stables and yard, with a gate out into the farm yard where they were hitched into their working harnesses and attached to the ploughs or harrows for the day's work. They would be led out of their yard through the gate by their leading reins and they had been

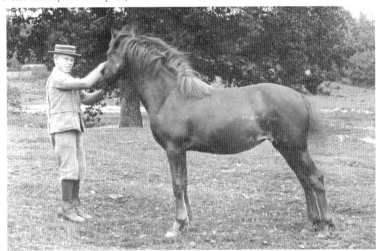

Richard Tame 1899

cleverly trained to shut gates themselves with one kick of a back hoof. Harry Tame was leading the carthorse out through the gate one-day in August 1900, not knowing that his youngest brother Richard was coming behind him. As the horse kicked back he missed the gate but the blow of his hoof caught young Richard full in the stomach. He collapsed in agony. By the time they had carried the boy up to his room and laid him on his bed, it was obvious that he was very seriously injured. The doctor was sent for, but was unable to do anything for him. Richard's life slowly ebbed away from him over the next two days, as a result of the internal bleeding caused by the violent injury. It was a terrible death, and an unthinkable tragedy for the whole family. Richard was the adored youngest son, 'baby' brother to Beatrice and her other brothers, Will and Harry.

The saddest outcome of this terrible event was the rift caused by the recriminations and blame directed at the eldest son, Harry, by Henry Tame, who blamed his eldest son for the death of the youngest son. He never really forgave Harry and it must have been a terrible burden for Harry Tame to carry for the rest of his life, even though it was only an unforeseen and tragic accident that can so easily happen on farms.

Richard was buried beside his beloved grandfather in the graveyard of the Baptist Chapel in Lyndhurst. The gravestone reads:

'In loving Memory of our Dickie Richard Thomas,
son of Henry and Letitia Tame,
who died August 15th 1900,
aged 12 years and 8 months.
"Be ye also ready,
For in such an hour as ye think not
the Son of Man Cometh."

After this tragedy I imagine that season gave way to season with no feelings of joy or exhilaration for Henry Tame the farmer and his sons, everything around them reminded them of the despair they all felt at the loss of young Richard. Beatrice and her mother must have lived in such gloom through the following months and years. Beatrice must have often wondered if she would ever escape from the sadness of their life at Bolderwood, which was perhaps only relieved by the summer visitors, their chapel friends and Miss May Forbes's long visits to Bolderwood Farm. The cheerful, sparkling busy and rewarding events that are recorded in Beatrice's diary of 1899 must have seemed like a long lost dream of an idyllic time never to be regained.

However, in the summer of 1905 three cheerful, sunburned and handsome young men strolled into Bolderwood farm, on a walking tour together, camping and exploring the Forest. They had all been schoolboys together at Tonbridge School; Carruthers, Airey and Page. Now they were veterans of the Boer War and Captain Page was a regular soldier, having gained a commission and decorations for his brave fighting. They asked if they could camp at Bolderwood for a few nights and, of course, were welcomed in the way that all walkers and visitors were at Bolderwood. Captain Page was captivated by the daughter of the farm, Beatrice, now aged 25 and a most attractive, accomplished and suitable young woman. They fell in love and Captain Page soon returned to the farm to ask for her hand in marriage. They were married the following year and Beatrice Tame, the farmer's daughter became the wife of Captain Page, who was by then on the staff of the Royal Military Academy at Sandhurst. She was carried away to a completely new life, leaving behind her beloved farm, the sadness and her happy younger life in the New Forest.

Her life thereafter is another story… waiting to be told.

Back in the Forest for a visit. Beatrice with her dog Peter in 1939

THE TAME FAMILY TREE
FROM 1796

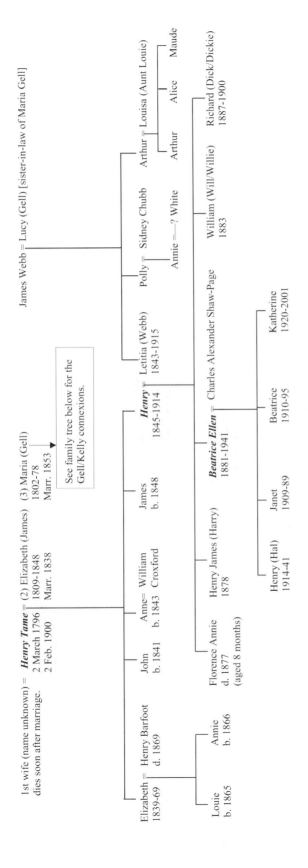

James Webb = Lucy (Gell) [sister-in-law of Maria Gell]

1st wife (name unknown) = **Henry Tame** = (2) Elizabeth (James) = (3) Maria (Gell)
dies soon after marriage. 2 March 1796 1809-1848 1802-78
2 Feb. 1900 Marr. 1838 Marr. 1853

See family tree below for the Gell/Kelly connexions.

Elizabeth = Henry Barfoot
1839-69 d. 1869

John
b. 1841

Anne= William
b. 1843 Croxford

James
b. 1848

Henry = Letitia (Webb)
1845-1914 1843-1915

Polly = Sidney Chubb

Annie =? White

Arthur = Louisa (Aunt Louie)

Louie
b. 1865

Annie
b. 1866

Florence Annie
d. 1877
(aged 8 months)

Henry James (Harry)
1878

Beatrice Ellen = Charles Alexander Shaw-Page
1881-1941

William (Will/Willie)
1883

Arthur

Alice

Maude

Richard (Dick/Dickie)
1887-1900

Henry (Hal)
1914-41

Janet
1909-89

Beatrice
1910-95

Katherine
1920-2001

John Gell = Maria (-?) [third wife of Henry Tame]

Maria Gell = Richard Kelly of Liverpool
b. 1852 marr. 1874

Sydney Appleton
b. 1880

Maria Gell = John Kemp Morris
b. 1876 marr. 1896

Florence Jane
b. 1879

These family trees are designed to show the basic relationships of those mentioned in the diary with sufficient detail to set each individual in his or her contextual relationship.

Biographical information

Barfoot, Annie (b. 1864 in Southampton, daughter of Henry Barfoot and Elizabeth, née Tame). As an orphan (both her parents died in 1869) she was taken in by her grandfather (Henry Tame, senior) and Maria, his third wife following whose death in 1878, she was 'adopted' by her aunt and uncle (Letitia and Henry Tame). She lived with the Tames at Bolderwood and is described in 1891 as an 'agricultural assistant' and in 1901 as a domestic helper and worker. It seems she had many tasks which included being a nanny to the Tame children. Although eighteen years older than her cousin Beatrice she seems to have been on very friendly terms with her.

Barfoot, Louie (b. 1865 in Southampton), Annie's sister who was also living at Bolderwood in 1901. She is described as a 'Lady's maid' and was employed by May Forbes in that capacity and sometimes travelled with her.

Barnard, William, house painter living in Silver Street, Emery Down (see 13 March).

Bingham, Miss. Evidently a close friend and companion of May Forbes. She stayed with her at Bolderwood (10 May). Often referred to in the dairy just as Miss B.

Briggs, Miss, a friend and companion to May Forbes. No further biographical information available.

Brookes (or Brooks), Miss Mary Ann, a lady companion and friend of May Forbes. Possibly she came from a farming family resident in Trent, Dorset.

Broomfield. Probably refers to Enos Edwin Broomfield, grocer, baker and corn merchant with premises in Lyndhurst. He was a member of the Baptist community.

Burrows, Eveline was a friend of Annie Croxford (b. Eling 1843), Henry Tame's sister (see Croxford, William).

Carlyon, Mrs (spelt Carlion in the diary). No proven biographical details available. It is just possible that Beatrice mistakenly wrote Mrs instead of Miss. If that is the case it could be one of the five daughters of the Rev. Edward Carlyon (1808-94) formerly of Shirley, Southampton and rector of Dibden 1860-94.

Chadband, the Rev. Mr. (23 May) Seemingly not a Church of England clergyman as his name cannot be discovered in the Crockford's *Clerical Directories* for 1889 and 1903. His name does not appear in *The Baptist Handbook, 1895*. He cannot be identified on the 1901 census, or in local trade directories. It seems therefore quite possible that the name may have been attributed satirically to the Rev Herbert Hughes, who lived at The Vicarage in Emery Down, having been taken from Dickens's *Bleak House* in which one of the characters is a clergyman, the Rev. Mr Chadband, described in *The Oxford Companion to English Literature* (1995) as 'the pious, eloquent humbug'.

Cheeseman, Alfred Henry (1865-1922) A Lyndhurst florist and greengrocer. His business was in the High Street but he also owned a market garden plot close to the Baptist Chapel. His wife was Frances (b.1865) and at the time of the diary they had four children, the two eldest, Alfred (Alfie) aged 5 and Frances (Fanny) aged 4, accompanied their father and his boy assistant to Bolderwood on 7 March. The business was continued under the ownership of Alfred until his death 1962. He had played an active role in the life of Lyndhurst, serving for a time as a parish councillor. He was a Baptist, serving as a deacon, and his funeral service was held in the Lyndhurst Baptist Church on Thursday, 18 October 1962.

Child, Miss lived in Southampton and was visited by Beatrice when she stayed with the Hendys (22 and 23 April). She visited the Tames on 29 June. No positive identification has been possible.

Chubb. Aunt Polly (25 March), Letitia Tame's sister and the wife of Henry Chubb of Bedford. Their daughter Annie, Beatrice's first cousin, is denoted as 'Annie (Bedford)' (28 April) to distinguish her from the other Annies in the diary and most particularly, Annie Barfoot. Henry Chubb was the proprietor of The Globe Hotel, Bedford

Clough, Florence. No biographical details available.

Compton, Neddy. An occasional assistant and labourer on Bolderwood Farm. No biographical information available.

Croxford, William Bailey (b.1844) was the husband of Annie Tame (b.1843), Beatrice's aunt, who he married in 1873. They had a son William Henry Croxford who was born in 1875. In the 1881 census he is recorded as an attendant at the British Museum. In the 1901 census he is recorded as a 'British Museum, Library Assistant'.

Duckworth. William resided at Beechwood in Copythorne parish from about 1840 until about 1860. He had employed Henry Tame, senior, as a gardener for around ten years from about 1842. The Miss Duckworth who visited the Tames on 19 April and again on 15 May, accompanied by her brother the Rev. William Arthur Duckworth (1829-1917), is a daughter of William. The Duckworths then owned the large estate called Orchardleigh, near Frome, in Somerset.

Dunn, Miss Beatrice. A lady companion of May Forbes (24 July). No further information known.

Evans, Mrs. Alice (b. 1872 in Halstead, Essex), the wife of Harry Evans who was the manager of George Frederick Saul's ironmongery business in Lyndhurst. Beatrice records dining with the Evans in company with Mr and Mrs Saul (5 April).

Epps, Mrs. Mary, née Lambert (b. 1853 in Retford, Notts.). She was a friend of the Tames and had close connexions with Walter Farrance (see below). She married William James Epps in 1882 in Ringwood (Walter Farrance was one of he witnesses). In 1901 she is recorded as being a business partner with Farrance in a nursery garden at Somerley View, Mill Lane, Ringwood which was close to Hurst Farm. Although there are eight separate references to her in the diary it has not been possible to discover the details of her relationship with the Tames. See also Lambert, Mr.

Evemy, Charles was born in Brockenhurst in 1844 and, at the time of the diary, lived with his wife, Charlotte and family at Merry Gardens, Burley. He was an Agister in the New Forest and became quite renowned locally for his work with and for the commoners (see 24 March). A photograph of him on horseback with two colleagues is reproduced in Kenchington, F.E., *The Commoners' New Forest* (1944), facing page 112, and there are a number of references to him in Pasmore, A., *Verderers of the New Forest* (1977). A portrait of him on horseback, now in the collections of the New Forest Museum and Library, was painted by Allen W. Seaby (1867-1953). One of his daughters visited Bolderwood on 13 August.

Eyre, Miss A., is Anna Sophia Penelope Eyre the eldest child of George Edward Eyre of the Warrens, Bramshaw. She was born in 1839, just six months before Elizabeth Tame, the eldest daughter of Henry Tame, senior, and his wife Elizabeth. Henry Tame was a gardener for G.E. Eyre so the two girls would have grown up together on the Warrens estate. Both were baptised at Bramshaw church. Her brother was the redoubtable New Forest commoner, Verderer and polemicist, George Edward Briscoe Eyre (1840-1922).

Farmer, Walter (b.1867) was a general dealer with a shop at Cadnam. He lived with his wife, Mary, and their five children. They were very much a local family.

Farrance, Walter (b.1840 in Hawkedown, Suffolk). He was serving as butler to John Turner-Turner of Avon Castle, Ringwood in 1881. In 1888 he married Sarah Carter who was employed as a maid in the same house. Later he joined William James Epps, a peat merchant, who ran a nursery garden in Ringwood. Following the death of Epps he became a business partner with his widow, Mary (née Lambert). There is a close connexion with the Tames and Beatrice several times refers to him as 'Uncle Farrance' and his wife, Sarah, as 'Auntie'. (see *e.g.* 5 and 30 April, 23 August). It has not been possible to discover the details of this relationship.

Forbes, James Staats (1823-1904) was a wealthy businessman and gentleman domiciled in London. He established a base at Bolderwood Farm in about 1890 (see 21 June) and this was to become the country retreat for his daughter May. He financed the construction of a large brick extension adjoining, and on the west side, of the farmhouse which was to be occupied by May Forbes and her friends. On his death in 1904 May received a direct bequest of £15,000 plus a quarter of the residue of his large estate, running to nearly half a million pounds. A portrait of J.S. Forbes was painted by Sir Hubert Herkomer who trained Frederick Golden Short (see below). His relationship with the Tames must have been very cordial for he sent a congratulatory telegram to Old Henry Tame on the occasion of his 103rd birthday (3 March). He stayed at Bolderwood 18 to 25 May and again, for May's birthday on 20 August, though he actually arrived on the following day. *The Dictionary of National Biography* provides biographical information. He was uncle to the famous artist, Stanhope A. Forbes.

Forbes, May (20 Aug. 1878 - 29 July 1962) was the illegitimate daughter of J.S. Forbes and a young lady of independent means. She inhabited separate quarters at Bolderwood Farm situated in the large brick built wing added to the west side of the farmhouse. She was well-educated and very self assured as would be expected from her position as the daughter of a well-established and wealthy businessman. May travelled widely as in the diary, at various times, she is recorded as being in Florence (9 March), Paris (29 April), Trent (27 May), London (9 June), the Lake District (6 July), Ware (21 July) and Germany (4 August). Being still a young woman she was always accompanied by one or another of her female friends and companions who shared her sojourns at Bolderwood. Her father spent a week with her in May and visited again on her birthday (20 August). Her quarters or apartments at Bolderwood seemed very much to be her rural retreat and she retained these premises until about 1924, well into the period when the farm lease was in the hands of William Tame. On relinquishing these premises she moved to a house, The Firs, in Stone Street, near Sevenoaks and later to Folkestone, where she died. Louie Barfoot was her lady's maid. May was a cousin of Stanhope Forbes (1857-1947), the renowned artist. She was godmother to Molly Hudson.

Fräulein. Probably the daughter of Fräu Keever, she was a personal friend and companion of Miss May Forbes.

French, Miss. (June 17) an older lady companion to May Forbes. No biographical information known.

Gailor. The Gailor family. It has not been possible to distinguish which of the Gailor families made the visits to Bolderwood, although Arthur, Fred and Tobe (Toby?) are specifically mentioned in the diary. It is a well-established local family.

Gibbins, H.E.J. (b.1864 in Stotfold, Beds), (5 March) took great interest in the gypsies in the New Forest and was head of the New Forest Good Samaritan Charity whose purpose was to assist those gypsy families most in need. He later wrote a book called *Gypsies of the New Forest and Other Tales* (1st edition, 1909). The Miss Gibbins referred to was one of his four daughters, probably Ada the eldest who was then aged 21. In about 1894 he moved to Burley establishing his home at Beacon Hill.

Goss, Herbert. No biographical information available.

Griffith, Richard W.S. (1852-1906) mentioned on 30 April. From 1874 he was the manager of the Schultz Gunpowder Factory at Eyeworth, Fritham. He was active in the Baptist church and made visits to Lyndhurst. Described in an obituary in the *Romsey Times*, 30 March 1906 as a very 'staunch Nonconformist'. See Ings, S., *Powder and Prayer* (2004).

Harcourt, Sir William Vernon (1827-1904), statesman, served in Gladstone's cabinet, becoming Chancellor of the Exchequer in 1886. Beatrice met him *en passant* on 9 September. He had moved into the Forest in 1883 and had built the huge house, Castle Malwood, on the site of a former forest lodge so he was a near neighbour of the Tames. He was a firm advocate in support of the preservation of the New Forest for he had fallen under its spell. He is quoted as saying on his visits to Malwood, "I never pass through this gate without feeling that I am coming to a haven of rest". Interestingly, he supported many of the aims of John Kensit in opposing the increasing ritualisation of the Church of England. (See Gardiner, A.G., *The Life of Sir William Harcourt*, 2 vols., 1923, *DNB* and Chadwick, O., *The Victorian Church*, vol. 2, 1970)

Hendy, Alfred (b.1870 in Southampton, d.1928) third son of Frederick and Mary Hendy. At the time of the diary he was living with his parents and family at 10 East Street, Southampton. Described in the 1901 census as a 'motor engineer' and as a 'worker at home'. He had close ties with the Tame family at Bolderwood. Familiarly referred to in the diary as Alf. He later ran the Hendy agricultural and motor vehicle business in Avenue Road, Brockenhurst but his home was St Cloud (later to become a hotel). He was tragically killed in a motor accident in 1928.

Hendy, Elizabeth (b.1872 in Southampton), eldest daughter of Frederick and Mary Hendy. Lived with her parents and family at 10 East Street. Close friend of the Tames and was known as Lizzie.

Hendy, Frederick Adolphus (b.1834 in Whitchurch, d.1923) was a businessman engaged in the cloth trade. Recorded as a clothier in the trade directories and also as a Lisle manufacturer and 'employer' in the 1901 census. He manufactured outdoor clothing for cyclists. His business premises were at 10 and 11 East Street. He was married to Mary and they had six children, namely, Frederick William, William E.W., Alfred Ernest, Percy Frank, Mary Jane and Elizabeth Annie. In 1903 the business was described as F.A. Hendy and Co. Ltd., outfitters, cycle and motor manufacturers with additional premises at York Buildings. He remarried after the death of his first wife. It was the eldest son, Frederick William (1865-1939), who established the present business of Hendy Holdings Ltd., which is still run by direct descendants.

Hendy, Mrs Fred (1871-1950) (21 April) was Eugenie Constance (née Rogers) the wife of Frederick William, the first son of Frederick and Mary Hendy. They were married in 1890. Ella Constance, who

Beatrice 'gave rides on her tricycle', was their first child born 1895 who lived to be 102, dying in 1998.

Hendy, Mary A. (b.1832 in Totton, d.1903), wife of Frederick. During the period of the diary she was often ill or indisposed, presumably with some chronic disorder as she survived until 1903. Close to the Tame family.

Hendy, Mary J. (b.1864), the eldest daughter and first child of Frederick and Mary Hendy (see 8 June).

Hendy, Percy (b. 1874 in Southampton), the youngest son of the Hendys. Described as cycle and motor salesman in the 1901 census. He appears to have been the founder of the Ford Motor franchise in Southampton, now trading as Hendy Ford Ltd.

Herbert, the Hon. Auberon (1838-1906), statesman, philosopher and traveller, came into the New Forest area when he took up residence at Ashley Arnewood in Milton parish in 1873. He purchased the Old House, Burley in 1886 where he became a firmly established and notable figure. He fought hard to preserve the natural beauty of the Forest and in 1888 held a long correspondence with the Hon. Gerald Lascelles about the activities of the Office of Woods and Forests in felling old hardwood trees (published for private circulation only). There is a tradition held by the descendants of the Tame family that his poem, *A Forest Secret*, describes Beatrice (quoted below the dedication in this book). His son, Auberon Herbert (later Lord Lucas) as a younger man, was prominent in breeding and showing New Forest ponies. He served as a captain in the Royal Flying Corps was killed in action in France in 1916, aged 40. (See *DNB* and Harris, S.H., *Auberon Herbert: Crusader for Liberty*, 1943).

Holloway, F. Identification uncertain.

Holloway, William was the Registrar of Births and Deaths and the Relieving, Vaccination and School Attendance Officer for the 2nd District of the New Forest Union (12 June).

Howard, Mr Edward Stafford (knighted in 1909 and known from thenceforth as Sir Stafford Howard) (1851-1916), Commissioner of Woods, Forests and Land Revenues, 1893-1912 (see 24 May).

Hughes, Mrs. Grace. The wife of the Rev. Herbert Thomas Hughes, vicar of Emery Down, 1880-1900 (see Chadband). She taught in the local Sunday school and was assisted occasionally by May Forbes, *e.g.* 4 June. They had a son, Sidney, baptised 4 July 1886 at Emery Down, who made visits to Bolderwood (see 26 July); he shortly afterwards joined the Royal Navy as an officer cadet. The Rev. H.T. Hughes resigned the living at Emery Down in 1900 and moved to St Luke's parish, West Norwood in that year. For an interesting, if anecdotal, view of Emery Down during the first part of Herbert T. Hughes' incumbency see Swayne, W.S., *Parson's Pleasure* (London, Blackwood 1934), 86-99.

Ings, Alfred (1852-1906) was a licensed victualler and hotel keeper who ran the Fox and Hounds in Lyndhurst. Some anecdotal details with a record of his tombstone inscription are recorded in *A Brief Jolly Change: The Diaries of Henry Peerless, 1891-1920* (Day Books, 2003), 115.

Kelly, Richard 'Uncle Dick' (1840-1919) was a building contractor in Liverpool. He was an alderman in the city and a Justice of the Peace. He married Maria Gell who was a daughter of Maria Gell who, after the death of her husband, Alfred, became the elder Henry Tame's third wife in 1853. There were three children born to the Kellys: Maria Gell Kelly (b.1876) who married the ship-owner John Kemp Morris (see below) in 1896, Florence Jane Kelly (b.1879) and Sydney Appleton Kelly (b.1880). He visited the Tames (30 March-10 April). In the 1901 census Richard Kelly and his wife are staying at a boarding house in Colwyn Bay.

Kelly, Sydney (b.1880) was the only son of Richard and Maria Kelly. Like his parents he was close to the Tame family and evidently a great favourite of Beatrice who was only a couple of years his junior (see her comments 10 April). He was visiting the Hendys in Southampton at the time of the 1901 census, so there was evidently a close link there also. He was trained as a surveyor and architect and designed the extension to Bolderwood for May Forbes in 1910 (the plans survive, TNA (PRO) F10/10).

Kensit, John (1853-1902) was an extreme evangelical and vehemently opposed to the growing ritualistic tendencies in the Church of England. The *DNB* describes him as a protestant agitator and as 'a sincere but narrow minded fanatic'. He remained an Anglican but travelled extensively around the country promoting his views (the "Kensit Crusade") and evidently they appealed to Beatrice Tame and her friends the Hendys (see 23 April). He also received some support from Sir William Harcourt whose campaign broadly reflected the same aims (Harcourt, W., *The Crisis in the Church*, 1899).

Lambert, Mr. He may be a relation of Mrs Epps, possibly a brother. Lives at Cocking, near Midhurst, Sussex. He visits Bolderwood with his daughters Annie (b.1892) and Ruth Elizabeth (1890), called Ruthie by Beatrice. In June his wife bore him a son (George), recorded by Beatrice on 6 June, "Ruthie Lambert wrote to tell me that she has another little brother". There may also be a connexion with the Tames through the Rev. Thomas Scamell who lived in the mid-1880s in, or near Steyning, Sussex. However, no positive identification has been possible.

Lane family. Francis (b. 1844 in Milford) and his wife Thamson (née Halsey), lived at Bolderwood Cottage, just a few hundred yards from Tames. Formerly, until 1883, he had been employed as a gamekeeper by David Fullerton, the tenant of Walhampton House in Boldre parish. He was then engaged by the Office of Woods as a Forest Keeper and moved to Bolderwood Cottage. Their eldest daughter, Thamson, had died in 1896, aged 15, and the diary refers to Beatrice making a primrose wreath for "Tammie's grave" (18 April). Mr Forbes found work for Thomas, one of their sons, at the railway carriage works at Ashford (20 June). The Lane children received their primary education at Emery Down School.

Lascelles, the Hon. Gerald (1849-1928) was appointed Deputy Surveyor of the New Forest in 1880. He lived with his wife Constance and family at the Queen's House in Lyndhurst. He was an enthusiastic and knowledgeable falconer. On retiring as Deputy Surveyor he wrote an important book relating to his life and experiences in the Forest entitled, *Thirty-Five Years in the New Forest* (1915). His visit to the Tames at Bolderwood on 24 May, accompanied by the Commissioner of Woods (see Howard), was primarily, it may be supposed, a business call. He has a grave in Lyndhurst Cemetery (restored by American and British falconers in May 2004).

Light, Richard (1829-99) was a farmer at Water Lane Farm, Totton. When Mr and Mrs Light visited with Mrs Light's mother on 30 May Beatrice described them as "a queer party". Was this prompted perhaps because of the 24 years disparity in the ages of Richard and his wife Fanny? Henry Tame visited Richard Light on 1 July, the evening he died, aged 70. He was buried at Eling on 4 July.

Macauley. (30 June) Probably a mistaken spelling. It is likely to have been Mrs Macleay whose residence was at Glasshayes (now Lyndhurst Park Hotel) in Lyndhurst. Her husband, Col. Alexander Macleay, CB (1843-1907), is commemorated on a mosaic inscription beneath a window in the south aisle of Lyndhurst church. The diarist probably misheard or misremembered the name.

Marshall, Mrs. Jane (b. 1833 in Ewshot, Hampshire) was a widow and sub-postmistress based at the Emery Down Post Office to which she was appointed in 1898. Her son Frank (b.1880), employed as a telegraphist at the Post Office, lived with her.

Maturin. The Rev. Benjamin (1816-1905), vicar of Lymington 1852-1905. He was appointed Dean of Lyndhurst Rural Deanery in 1892 (see 22 June). Further details, including a photographic portrait, may be found in Bostock, C. and Hapgood, E., *The Church in Lymington* (King, Lymington 1911).

Maturin. The Rev. Charles (b.1866), youngest son of Benjamin Maturin, entered the church as deacon in 1890. He was appointed to the curacy of Minstead in 1892. He also, on occasion, preached or served in other ways at Christ Church, Emery Down. He moved in 1899 to Woburn to serve as curate there (see 11 March). He returned to the New Forest area when he was installed as vicar of Colbury in 1901.

May, Edward (b. 1849 in Lymington), Lyndhurst watchmaker with premises in the High Street, adjoining the Shorts. Beatrice took her brooch to him to have the rivet replaced, see 17 Aug. He married Ann Rogers (b. 1847 in Mottisfont) in 1873.

May, Florence (Florrie) (b.1883), daughter of Edward and Ann May of Lyndhurst.

May, Lillian (Lily or Lillie) (b.1887), youngest daughter of Edward and Ann May.

Mills, Harry "Brusher" (1840-1905) was renowned as a snake catcher in the New Forest and still remains a figure of great interest. Visited the Tames on 31 May and 7 June. (See Stagg, D.J., *Snake Catchers of the New Forest* (NFA, 1983).

Morant, Mrs (15 August). This probably refers to Flora Jane Morant (1832-1915), widow of John Morant (1825-99), lord of the manor of Brockenhurst, who had died only two months earlier and whose funeral took place at Brockenhurst church on 6 June at which the Rev. Benjamin Maturin officiated.

Morris, John 'Jack' Kemp (b.1869) in 1894 married Maria Gell Kelly (b.1868). She was a granddaughter of Henry Tame, senior's, third wife, Maria (née Gell). Morris, trading as John K. Morris, owned trading vessels that sailed around the Welsh, Irish and West Country coasts from Liverpool. He is recorded as a ship owner and a ship broker in the 1901 census. Richard Kelly loaned money to his son-in-law to help him in his maritime business ventures. The Tames also had invested money in his company but the enterprise failed and their investments were lost (for further details see the Prologue and in Fenton, R.S., *Mersey Rovers* (World Ship Society, 1997), pp.161-164).

Otten, Miss Lizzie Mary (b.1878), a dressmaker who lived with her widowed mother in Wellands Road, Lyndhurst (see 5 April and 5 July).

Palmer, Dr Edwin (b.1825), Archdeacon of Oxford and a renowned biblical scholar. He must have known Dean H.G. Liddell of Christ Church, Oxford, the father of Alice (in Wonderland), who in 1880 was to marry Reginald Hargreaves of Cuffnells Park, Lyndhurst and where she was living at the time of the diary. Curiously enough in 1881 Lewis Carroll was lodging with Dr Palmer in Oxford. He visited the Tames on 4 July.

Payne. There are several Payne families living in the Lyndhurst, Minstead and Emery Down areas and it has not been possible to identify which is referred to in the diary. Several Paynes were active in the Lyndhurst Baptist community and one had been a minister; a few have headstones in the Baptist churchyard. The Paynes are engaged in the building trade: Albert Payne of Emery Down is a 'bricklayer' (and he has a daughter Annie, see 14 March), William Payne of Lyndhurst is a 'builder' (his wife Adeline is recorded as a 'draper'). Could this be the Mrs Payne Beatrice visited on 31 May 'to get some lace for my dress'? Mr F.P. Payne of Emery Down also a 'builder'.

Pechell (Pechil), Mr and Mrs. He is likely to be Thomas Pechell (b.1836) who was verger at All Saints Church, on the corner of East Street, Southampton (destroyed by enemy action, 1940), and his wife. In the 1881 census he is recorded as a 'Missionary to Seamen' and was at that time residing at Ipswich.

Petty, Murray (b.1862 in Bransgore). He was the son of a farmer and that, no doubt, accounts for the connexion with the Tame family.

Retford. Mrs Jane (b.1835) and her husband William (b.1829) were employed by the Hon. Auberon Herbert, first at Ashley Arnewood in Milton parish and later at the Old House, Burley. Whilst living at Milton she had two daughters, Annie (b.1861) and Jane (b.1870) and two sons, Richard (b.1872) and William (1875-1970), the latter became world famous as a maker of bows for stringed instruments. He wrote a book on the subject entitled, *Bows and Bow Makers* (1964).

Robinson, Sarah (1835-1915) was a distinguished lady philanthropist, known as "The Soldiers' Friend" because of her work for the soldiers at Aldershot: she later founded the Soldiers' Institute at Portsmouth. In 1892 she moved to Burley where she purchased from Woodman Edward Sims a parcel of land on Blake's Plot. On this land she had a special single storey timber house constructed which she called "The Hut" and which Beatrice visited on 27 April. From these premises over a number of years she edited a monthly journal entitled *Ready* which contains regular accounts of the Portsmouth Institute. Her autobiography, *"My Book"* – *A Personal Narrative* (1914), contains a short description of Henry Tame, senior, with a photograph of him.

Sampson, Mr, was a missionary who sent his journal, which detailed his overseas missions, to Letitia Tame to correct and transcribe (see 4 March). He is not recorded in *The Baptist Handbook 1895* and no other information has been uncovered.

Saul, Mrs Clara (b.1856) and her husband, George Frederick Saul (b.1852). He owned a substantial and successful ironmongery and hardware business at 89-90 High Street, Lymington (the business survived until 1938). He also ran a branch in Lyndhurst (see 5 April) under the management of Harry Evans (see above).

Scamell, the Rev. Tom Webb (1857-1929), Baptist minister at Lyndhurst from 1890 to 1928. He trained for the pastorate at Spurgeon College, London and was appointed to his first ministry at Barton (1883-89). The chapel there had been built by Mrs John Villiers Dent of Barton Court. Scamell later became pastor at Ashley but only for a few months during 1889-90. He lived with his wife, Catherine (née Hayward), at the Lyndhurst manse called Meadowlands. There were four sons: William Hayward (b.1880), Ernest Edward (b.1882), Philip Henry (b.1883) and Thomas Lucas (b.1885). He raised the status of the Baptist community in Lyndhurst and increased the assets of the chapel. In addition to these achievements he was much involved in the wider community serving for several years as chairman of the parish council, as a manager of the C. of E. school and also on the local burial board. During his pastorate at Barton he made a visit to Hordle to see Mary Ann Girling, the 'Mother' of the Children of God (otherwise known as the New Forest Shakers). It is recorded that he asked her searching theological questions regarding her claim to immortality, but was unsatisfied and left unconvinced by her assertions. The Rev. Tom Scamell lies in Lyndhurst cemetery. (Scamell is sometimes spelt Scammell, however, the single 'm' is correct as can be confirmed by his signature on his marriage certificate, 6 January 1880 and in the Baptist Church Minute Book.)

Shaw, Mr., described by Beatrice as "Missionary to the Gypsies" (14 March). There is no biographical information available.

Short, Frederick Golden (1863-1936). Only son of John G. Short (see below). He never married. Like his father he was an accomplished photographer working in the family studios in Lyndhurst, but became much more renowned as an artist, painting mainly landscapes in both watercolours and oils. He received professional training under (Sir) Hubert (von) Herkomer and at the Southampton School of Art. He was an active member and organist at the Lyndhurst Baptist church. He lies in the Baptist churchyard where his memorial stone records him as a "New Forest Artist". During the period of the diary he made several visits to Bolderwood and was on good terms with the Tame family. He may also have had connexions with the Forbes through Stanhope Forbes (cousin of May Forbes), the artist. He certainly made a special visit to Bolderwood to photograph May Forbes and her dog, Pumpkin (28 July).

Short, John Golden (b. in Lyndhurst in 1832). He owned the chemist shop in the High Street, Lyndhurst. He was an accomplished photographer whose works were very highly esteemed and earned many testimonials. Short's photographs are much admired to the present day. By the 1890s he was trading primarily as a photographer and his business was known as the New Forest Photographic Studio. He was prominent in the affairs of the Lyndhurst Baptist community. At the time of the diary he was a widower living with his son Frederick Golden Short and his sister, Mary Ann Short (b.1852). (See 12 June).

Stares (Stairs in the diary), George (b.1849) was a farmer at Minstead Lodge Farm (7 August). This farm was later taken as a tenancy by Henry James Tame.

Starling, Miss B. (24 July) Another of May Forbes's lady companions. No information on this lady has been discovered.

Tame, Henry (1796-1900), grandfather of Beatrice Tame the diarist. He was a gardener for the Eyre family at the Warrens and moved from there to become a gardener for William Duckworth at Beechwood in Bartley (then in Eling parish) in about 1842. His son Henry Tame was born there 15 November 1845. Often referred to as either Old Henry or Old Tame. See the Prologue for further Tame family details.

Tame, Henry (1845-1914), father of Beatrice Tame. Married Letitia Webb and moved to Hill Farm, Thorney Hill (Bransgore parish). Their first child, Florence Annie, was born there in May 1877 and died the following December. She was buried at Bransgore, 8 December 1877. Their second child, Henry James, was baptised at Bransgore 20 November 1878. On leaving Hill Farm Henry became tenant farmer at Bolderwood on 25 March 1879. See Introduction and Prologue for further information.

Tame, Letitia (née Webb) (1843-1915) married Henry Tame. She died on 9 January 1915 only five weeks after her husband. Both are interred in the Baptist Church graveyard in Lyndhurst. (See Prologue)

Tame, Henry James (b.1878), eldest son of Henry and Letitia Tame and Beatrice's eldest brother. Generally called Harry in the diary. (See Prologue)

Tame, Beatrice Ellen (1881-1941), the diarist. Only surviving daughter of Henry and Letitia Tame. She was their first child to be born at Bolderwood. Generally called Bee (Sumner just refers to her as B, "Does B. read to you?" a question directed at old Henry Tame). (See Prologue and Introduction)

Tame, William John (b.1883) baptised at Christchurch, Emery Down on 18 May 1883. Generally referred to in the diary as either Will or Willie. After his father's death in 1914 the lease of Bolderwood Farm was assigned to him. (See Prologue and Introduction.)

Tame, Richard Thomas (1887-1900). Beatrice's youngest brother. Baptised at Christchurch, Emery Down on 5 March 1887. Referred to in the diary as either Dick or Dickie. See Epilogue for details of his short life.

Tame, James (b.1848), youngest son of Henry Tame senior and brother of Henry and uncle to Beatrice.

Taylor, Miss Laura, a lady companion to May Forbes. No biographical details are known.

Taylor, Thomas (b.1843) had a farm at Winsor, the Tames had regular dealings with him, mainly regarding horses. The death of his wife, Elizabeth, is referred to by Beatrice on 23 June, when she states she "died last Friday", *i.e.* on the 16 June. She was buried at Copythorne on the 18th, aged 55 years.

Venvell, Hubert and Herbert (twins, b. 1877 in Milton-under-Wychwood) younger brothers of Thomas. Presumably they joined their brother Thomas after he had established his business in Emery Down.

Venvell, Thomas (b. 1868 in Milton-under-Wychwood) first appears in Lyndhurst in 1891 as a grocer's assistant to Harriet Broomfield whose shop was in the High Street. He was then aged 23. In September 1893, as a newly married man, he took over the business of the shop and Post Office at Emery Down. The parish magazine commented, "We hope they will find business grow and prosper". In this he was following in his father's footsteps as he was Post Master, grocer and baker at Ascott in Oxford. Both Thomas and his wife made donations to the school. At the same time, as grocer, he also supplied refreshments to the school; his bill for the school treat in September 1899 came to £1 13s. 4d.

Venvell, Mrs., the wife of Thomas (née Alice Maud Foot, b.1871). It appears there were no children of this marriage during their residence in Emery Down. They had returned to Oxfordshire before 1901.

Venvell, William. In September 1893 he set up business in Emery Down as a carrier running to and from Southampton on Tuesdays, Thursdays and Saturdays. His conveyance departed from Emery Down Post Office at 9 a.m. on those days and returned from Southampton at 4.30 p.m. He was appointed sidesman at Emery Down Church in 1893 and in January 1899 it is recorded that he "most kindly drove some of the choir to Lyndhurst Road". His relationship with Thomas Venvell is not clear.

Webb, Alice, Arthur and Maude were the three children of Arthur Webb, Letitia Tame's brother, and his wife Louie, referred to in the diary as 'Aunt Louie'. They lived at Surbiton. Arthur stayed at Bolderwood on 19 August after making the 92-miles cycle run from Surbiton to Bolderwood in 6 hours.

White. Dr Barrington (b. 1850) lived with his wife, Mary, and their three daughters at The Evergreens, Romsey Road, Lyndhurst. In addition to being a general medical practitioner he was also the local medical officer and vaccinator for the Lyndhurst District and the New Forest Union Workhouse at Ashurst (see 22 June).

BIBLIOGRAPHY and SOURCES

Primary sources

Census returns (microfiche/microfilm)

Census 1851 (HO 107/1668)

Census 1881 (RG11/1202)

Census 1891 (RG12/0910)

Census 1901 (RG13/1050)

Parish registers (microfiche) for:

Boldre

Bramshaw

Bransgore

Copythorne

Eling

Emery Down (marriages)

Emery Down Burial and Baptismal registers (originals)

Lyndhurst

Minstead

Lyndhurst Baptist Church Minute Book

Minstead Tithe Map and Apportionment 1840

General Register Office Indexes of Births Marriages and Deaths (microfiche)

TNA (PRO) F10/10 (Office of Woods, Bolderwood file)

Probate Office

Will of James Staats Forbes (1904)

Will of May Forbes (1962)

Private correspondence

Molly Hudson

Websites

British Library

IGS Family Search

FreeBMD

TNA (PRO) 1901 census

Primary printed sources

Baptist Handbook 1895

Craven & Co's *Hampshire Directory* 1857

Crockford's *Clerical Directories*, 1898 and 1903

Kelly's Directories for Hampshire 1890, 1895, 1899 and 1920

Newspapers

The Hampshire Chronicle (for the year 1899)

The Salisbury and Winchester Journal (for the year 1899)

The Hampshire Independent, 12 December 1914

Secondary printed sources

Babey, G. and Roberts, P., *Lyndhurst: A Brief History and Guide* (Ashurst, Nova Foresta, 2003)

Bostock, C. and Hapgood, E., *The Church in Lymington* (Lymington, King, 1912)

Chadwick, O., *The Victorian Church* (Black, 1970)

Coatts, M (editor), *Cuckoo Hill: The Book of Gorley* (Dent, 1987)

Dictionary of National Biography (for Forbes, Harcourt, Herbert, and Kensit)

Drabble, M (editor), *The Oxford Companion to English Literature* (1995 edition)

F.A. Hendy & Lennox Ltd., *100 Years of the Hendy Group* (Hendy 2001)

Fenton, R.S., *Mersey Rovers* (World Ship Society 1997)

Gardiner, A.G., *The Life of Sir William Harcourt*, 2 vols (London, Constable 1923)

Hardcastle, F., *Aspects of a New Forest Village: Records of Burley* (Spalding 1987)

Harris, S.H., *Auberon Herbert: Crusader for Liberty* (Williams & Norgate 1943)

Ings, S., *Powder and Prayer* (printed privately, 2004), esp. pp.24-30 for R.W.S. Griffith.

Jackman, R., *Lyndhurst Past and Present*, Books I-V (Lyndhurst, 1969-76)

Kenchington, F.E., *The Commoners' New Forest* (1944)

Lascelles, G., *Thirty-five Years in the New Forest* (Arnold 1915)

Manning, R., 'Origins of the Golden Short Family', *Nova Foresta Magazine*, Vol. 3, No.3 (Autumn 1997), 22-25.

Mays, J. O'D., *The New Forest Book: An Illustrated Anthology* (Burley, 1989)

New Forest Magazine, Vol. 42, No.11, Nov. 1929 (under 'Lyndhurst').

Parkes, G., 'Rev. Edward Carlyon and All Saints Church, Dibden', *Waterside Heritage* No. 21

Robinson, S., *"My Book" - A Personal Narrative* (London, Partridge, 1914)

Saunders, N., 'By the Lin River, they fought TB in the New Forest: The Story of Linford Sanatorium' *Hampshire Magazine*, Vol. 32, No. 12 (Oct. 1992), 38-40.

Sumner, H., *The Book of Gorley* (Chiswick 1910)

Swayne, W.S., *Parson's Pleasure* (London, Blackwood, 1934)

Vanity Fair, 22 Feb. 1900

Walford, M, 'The Short Family in Lyndhurst' in *Pollards, People and Ponies* (1979), 21-34

Woods, C., *Dictionary of British Art.* Vol. IV. *Victorian Painters* 1. The Text (Antique Collectors' Club 1995) under 'Forbes', 'Herkomer' and 'Short'.

INDEX

Relationships are to the diarist. Numbers refer to dates, e.g. 17/5 is 17 May.
Close family names are not individually indexed because of their very frequent (often almost daily) occurrence.

birthday, 6/3, 12/4, 15/4, 15/8
Bobby Bank's Bodderment, 4/4
boil, 25/3
Bolderwood, 9/4
Bolderwood Cottage, 22/5
Bolderwood Hill, 2/5
Boscombe, 15/8, 23/8
Bourne School, 15/7
Bournemouth, 4/4, 5/4, 7/5, 3/6, 31/7, 9/9
Bowden-Smith, Mr., 13/7
brake (bicycle), 25/5, 27/5
brandy, 24/8
Bratley Green, 13/7, 14/7
Bratley Hill, 6/5
Briggs, Miss E., 21/6, 23/6, 29/6, 30/6
Brockenhurst, 6/4, 7/5, 25/5, 1/6, 10/6, 20/6, 21/6, 21/8
brooches, 17/8
Brooker, Rev., 12/7
Brookes, Mary Ann, 30/5, 3/6, 4/6, 5/6, 6/6
Broomfields, 19/4, 20/4, 7/8
bronchitis, 21/3
Brownie, 16/5, 17/5, 9/7
Browning, Mr., 10/7
Browns, 14/3
Brusher (Mills), 31/5, 7/6
Burgess, Mr., 8/5
Burley, 3/4, 16/4, 24/4, 29/4, 1/5, 7/5, 3/6, 4/8, 16/8
bus, 24/4
Bushharrow, 10/4
Bushy Bratley, 15/7, 16/7

Cadnam, 7/9
camera, 22/5, 9/6
candlestick, 12/4
Canterton, 3/4.
carriage, 3/6, 20/6, 30/6
Carlion (Carlyon), Mrs., 18/4
Carlyle (Thomas), 17/4
cauliflowers, 11/5
Centenary Farthings, 5/4
Chadband, the Rev. Mr and Mrs., 23/5
chain letter, 14/3.
Champagne, 23/5
Chandler, 12/5, 23/6
Chapel, 5/3, 12/3, 19/3, 22/3, 2/4, 9/4, 16/4, 23/4, 24/4, 30/4, 7/5, 21/5, 28/5, 4/6, 11/6, 2/7, 9/7, 12/7, 16/7, 23/7, 30/7,
    6/8, 13/8, 20/8, 3/9
Cheeseman, Alfred (Alfie), 7/3, 28/3, 16/6
Cheeseman, Frances (Fannie), 7/3, 28/3
Cheeseman, Mr. Alfred Henry, 7/3, 28/3, 16/6
Cheeseman, Mrs. Frances, 26/5
chestnut mare (horse), 14/3, 3/4, 10/4, 18/4, 19/4, 20/4, 25/4, 26/4, 30/4, 20/5, 13/6, 14/6, 19/6, 7/7
cherries, 13/7
Child, Miss, 19/4, 22/4, 23/4, 29/6
Child, Mrs., 29/6
chocolates, 30/6
choir, 30/4, 13/8

church, 11/5, 21/5, 26/5, 5/6, 19/7, 19/8
Christian plums, 5/9
Clark, Fred, 22/5
Cleveland, Mr., 22/5
Clipper (bicycle), 25/5, 26/5
Clough, Miss, 3/4, 15/7, 19/7
Clough, Miss Florence, 15/7
Clough, Mrs., 15/7
coal, 7/6
Cochrane, Mr., 13/4
colds, 24/3, 17/5, 21/6, 30/6
Cole Bridge, 28/5, 29/5
Cole(s), Mr and Mrs., 14/6, 21/6, 7/7
collar, sable, 21/6
Collins, Rev., 12/7
colt hunting, 31/7, 5/8
colt-lambing, 24/3
communion, 7/5, 2/7, 9/7, 16/7, 30/7
Commissioner of Woods, 24/5
composer, grand, 24/8
Compton Arms, 15/5
Compton, Neddy, 4/5, 5/5, 16/6
Corke, Mrs., 8/9
Corke, Neville, 8/9, 9/9
Cornwall, 6/5, 10/5, 17/6
Coronation Day, 29/6
Cranley, 13/5
cricket, 22/5, 14/6, 13/7, 17/7, 7/8
crippled, 16/8
crocklette, 17/4, 10/6
croquet, 1/9
Crystal Palace, 11/4
cyclamen, 28/3

Dada (Mr Henry Tame), frequent references.
Davies, Mr and Mrs. W., 25/7
Davies, Nellie, 25/7
Davis, Mr and Mrs., 7/9
Davis, William, 20/7
Deacon, Jim, 18/7
Deacon, Mr., 13/6
Dean, 18/7
deer, fallow, 15/7
derder/der/ders, 7/6, 21/6
Devon, 10/5, 20/7
diary, 8/4, 9/4, 24/11
Dick (Richard, brother), frequent references.
Dick, Uncle, 30/3, 31/3, 7/4, 10/4, 1/5
doll(s), 3/4, 2/5, 19/6, 25/7, 26/7
donkey cart, 25/7
Duckworth, Miss, 19/4, 15/5
Duckworth, Mr. A., 13/5, 15/5, 29/6
Dunn, Miss Beatrice, 24/7, 26/7, 28/7, 30/7, 31/7, 2/8, 4/8, 8/8
Dunning, Mrs and Miss, 7/8

East Street (Southampton), 24/4

Easter Egg, 20/3
Eastleigh, 10/5
Egerton, Mrs., 2/6
Egerton, the Rev. George, 2/6, 14/6, 12/7
Eldridge, Georgie, 24/3
elect, two of the, 20/5
Eling, vicar of, 7/7
Elliot, Miss, 15/7
Emery Down, 5/4, 19/4, 18/5, 22/5, 29/5, 4/6, 5/6, 18/6, 20/6, 3/7, 21/7, 26/7, 19/8
Emery, Mr. and Mrs., 23/5, 16/8
enamelling, 12/4
Epps, Mrs., 18/3, 5/4, 30/4, 18/5, 20/5, 13/6, 23/8, 1/9
Epsom Salts, 18/5
Evangeline, 15/4
Evans, Amy, 3/4
Evans, Mr., 3/4, 5/4, 26/4
Evans, Mrs., 3/3, 5/3, 8/3, 15/3, 3/4, 5/4, 8/4, 14/4, 15/4, 26/4, 13/5, 23/5, 26/5, 31/5, 7/6, 10/7, 21/7, 25/7
Evans, Stanley, 10/7
Eveline, 29/4, 2/5, 9/5, 16/6, 5/7, 11/8, 12/8, 21/8
Evemy, Mr. Charles, 24/3, 4/5
Evemy, Miss, 13/8
Eyer, Miss Anna, 26/3, 1/4, 25/4, 29/6

fainted, 9/4, 20/8
Family Friend, 1/6
Farmer(s), Mr. Walter, 15/4, 17/4, 29/4, 1/5, 17/6, 9/8
Farrance, Mr., 5/4, 30/4, 19/5, 23/8
Farrance, Mrs., 18/3, 23/8
Felixstowe, 4/8
Fenely, Mr and Mrs., 19/6
Firemen's dinner, 5/4
Fleet, Mr. William, 18/5, 22/5, 25/5, 21/8, 23/8
Florence, 9/3
flour, 15/6
Flower Service, 5/6
foot pump, 16/8
Forbes, James Staats, 3/3, 6/3, 7/3, 18/5, 22/5, 24/5, 25/5, 20/6, 21/6, 15/8, 22/8, 23/8
Forbes, May (Miss May), 7/3, 9/3, 11/3, 25/3, 27/3, 28/3, 2/4, 3/4, 15/4, 29/4, 4/5, 8/5, 9/5, 10/5, 11/5, 12/5, 14/5, 16/5,
    17/5, 18/5, 20/5, 21/5, 23/5, 24/5, 25/5, 26/5, 30/5, 31/5, 2/6, 3/6, 4/6, 5/6, 6/6, 9/6, 10/6, 12/6, 15/6, 17/6, 18/6, 19/6,
    20/6, 21/6, 23/6, 29/6, 30/6, 1/7, 2/7, 3/7, 4/7, 5/7, 6/7, 17/7, 21/7. 22/7, 24/7, 25/7, 26/7, 27/7, 28/7, 29/7, 30/7, 31/7,
    1/8, 2/8, 4/8, 10/8, 15/8, 16/8, 17/8, 18/8, 19/8, 20/8, 21/8, 22/8, 23/8, 7/9, 8/9
Forbes, Mrs., 5/6, 18/6, 21/6
Forman, Mrs., 5/9
Frampton, Mr., 7/8
Fräulein, 15/8, 16/8, 17/8, 19/8, 10/8, 7/9, 8/9
Freak (horse), 15/4
Freeman, Mr., 10/7
Fremington, 10/5
French, Miss, 17/6, 18/6, 19/6, 20/6, 21/6
French Revolution, 17/4
freesias, 28/3
fresco (Lord Leighton's), 28/4
fresh girl, 22/7
Fritham, 1/6, 2/6, 10/8
frost, 12/4

Gailor, Arthur, 11/3, 12/5, 17/5
Gailor, Fred., 11/3
Gailor, Tobe, 5/4, 6/4, 11/5, 17/5, 1/6, 8/8, 15/8, 23/8
Gailors, 1/6
gathering, 21/3, 3/5, 15/5, 16/6
George/Georgie, 14/4, 15/4, 18/4, 20/4, 21/4, 30/7, 15/8, 16/8, 23/8, 6/9, 7/9, 8/9
Germans, 7/5
Germany, 23/5, 4/8
Gibbins, Mr (H.E.J.) and Miss, 5/3, 1/6
Gilbert, Mrs., 21/5
ginger beer, 6/6
Girls Own, 21/7
glass houses, 28/3
Globosia (Buddleia globosa), 17/6
Godshill, 9/5
Goff, Mr., 9/6, 5/8, 9/8
Goss, Mr Herbert and Mrs., 15/7
Golding, Mr., 3/4, 7/5, 11/5, 30/5
Graphic, 23/5
Grandfather, The, 2/4
Grandpa (Old Henry Tame)
Grieg (Edvard), 10/6
Griffith(s), R.W.S, 30/4
Gulliver, Mr., 18/4, 20/4
gun, 4/5, 6/6, 7/6, 8/6, 13/6, 14/6
Gypsies, 14/3

Hahn, Oscar, Mr and Mrs., 7/5
Halfpenny Green, 7/7, 15/7
Harcourt, Sir William, 7/9
harmonium, 8/5, 28/5, 13/8
Harris, Miss M., 4/3, 15/4, 19/4, 26/4, 27/4
Harry/Henry (brother), frequent references.
headache, 29/6, 19/7
Hedges, Miss, 9/4, 13/5, 23/5
Hedges, Mrs., 13/5
Hendy, Alfred (Alf), 10/3, 14/4, 24/4, 27/4, 28/4, 6/5, 7/5, 8/5, 24/5, 29/5, 30/5, 2/6, 3/6, 1/7, 5/7, 6/7, 11/7, 6/8, 14/8, 15/8, 6/9, 9/9
Hendy, Elizabeth (Lizzie), 19/4, 21/4, 22/4, 23/4, 27/4, 29/5, 2/6, 23/6, 29/6, 28/7, 15/8
Hendy, Mary, 8/6, 10/6, 14/8, 23/8
Hendy, Mr. 21/4, 23/4
Hendy, Mrs., 3/3, 17/3, 24/3, 30/3, 7/4, 15/4, 16/4, 17/4, 21/4, 22/4, 23/4, 24/4, 26/4, 27/4, 28/4, 5/5, 6/5, 12/5, 26/5, 2/6, 16/6, 7/7, 9/7, 11/7, 14/7, 21/7, 11/8, 8/9
Hendy, Mrs. Fred, 21/4
Hendy, Percy, 10/3 23/4,
Hendys, 9/6, 23/6
Henry Clark, 3/7
Herbert, the Hon. Auberon, 29/6, 10/8
Hill Top, 1/7
Hilliar, Miss, 2/5, 13/5
Hinchesley, 8/8
Hole, Miss, 19/4
holiday, 10/4, 3/5, 10/5, 13/5, 30/7, 7/8
Holloway, Mr. F., 5/4
Holloway, Mr. W., 12/6
Holly, Mrs., 7/6

Holmsley, 16/8
Hotel, 6/9
hounds, 30/3, 3/4, 18/4
Howard, Mr., 24/5
Hughes, 20/8
Hughes, the Rev., 23/5
Hughes, Mrs., 23/5, 25/5, 26/5, 4/6, 5/6, 1/8
Hughes, Sidney, 26/7, 31/7, 1/8, 18/8, 21/8
hunt, 30/3
Hut, The, 27/4
Hutchings, Mr., 24/3
Hythe, 14/8

In His Steps, 12/4
infirmary, 6/3
influenza, 18/3, 30/4
Ing, Mr., 27/5
Ings, 20/6
inkstand, 23/5
Inwood, Mr., 2/6
Isle of Man, 1/5

jam, 15/7
James, Miss, 11/3
James, Uncle, 10/3, 11/8, 1/9, 4/9
Jeanes, Mr., 4/8
Jeanes, Mrs., 9/7
Jeanes, Willie, 3/3, 5/4
Jeffreys, Mr and Mrs., 29/6
Jenkins, Mr and Mrs., 17/8
Jessie/Jesse (pony), 1/4, 8/5, 18/7, 19/7, 20/7, 27/7
Jock (pony), 13/6
Joey/Joe (pony), 20/5, 23/5, 26/5, 1/6, 6/6, 12/6, 14/6, 15/6, 11/7, 17/7, 21/7, 30/7, 12/8, 21/8, 4/9
Jonathan Merle, 2/4, 9/4
Jones, Auntie, 26/4
Jones (Edwin), 22/4
Joy, Rev., 12/7
juniper, 9/4

keep (Henry's), 4/3
Keever, Fräu, 4/8
Kelly, Auntie, 27/5, 31/5
Kelly, Sydney A., 30/3, 1/4, 5/4, 6/4, 7/4, 8/4
Kelly, Richard 'Uncle Dick', 30/3, 5/4
Kensit, John, 23/4
Keswick, 6/7
King, Mr., 11/6
Kingston Pound, 4/5, 5/5
kitten, 12/4, 12/5
kitchen, 13/4, 6/7
knife, hay, 5/5

laburnum, 25/5, 31/5
Lady Cross, 19/7
Lambert, Annie,
Lambert, Mr., 25/3, 13/4, 18/4, 24/4, 25/4, 27/4, 28/4, 2/5, 3/5

May, Florrie, 28/5, 29/5, 17/6, 12/7
May, Lilly/Lilie, 5/3, 28/5, 29/5, 12/7
May, Miss (see Forbes, May)
May, Mr. Edward, 28/5, 17/8
May, Mrs. Ann, 13/5
May, Sydney, 2/9
meet (hunting), 3/4, 18/4
Meeting, 7/8
meringues, 10/5, 25/5, 4/7
Merino petticoat, 15/4
Merry (pony), 17/7, 19/7, 31/7, 9/8
merrys, 10/7, 18/7
milk/milking, 2/6
Millard, Mr., 8/3
Millbrook, 10/3, 21/4
Milliford, 29/5
Mills, 6/7, 8/8, 15/8, 23/8
Minstead, 11/3, 5/4, 16/6
mission, 18/4
missionaries, 4/3
Molyneux, family, 4/7
Money Hills, 28/5
Morant, Mrs., 15/8
Mornee (pony), 1/5, 28/5, 2/6
Morris, Miss, 18/6, 20/6
Morris, Mr., 7/3, 10/5
motelle, 29/5
Mother (see Mama)
motor tricycle, 10/3
Murray, A., 19/4
Museum (British), 21/7

needlework, 7/6, 8/6, 27/7, 5/8
Nelson, Lord, 25/4
New South Wales, 14/3

Oakley, 25/4, 4/8
Ocknell Pond, 20/6, 22/8
orchard, 16/7
organ, 11/6, 18/6
organ, American, 9/6, 15/6, 18/6
Otten, Miss, 5/4, 5/7

Padstow, 6/5, 8/5, 10/5
Paint/painting, 6/3, 7/3, 8/3, 9/3, 11/3, 14/3, 15/3, 16/3, 20/3, 22/3, 25/3, 13/4, 14/4, 17/4, 2/5, 3/7, 6/7
Palmer, Dr. Edwin, 4/7
Paris, 29/4
Parker, Auntie, 26/4
Parkstone, 14/7
partridge, 18/7
Payne, Annie, 14/3
Payne, Mrs., 12/3, 5/4, 26/4, 2/5, 13/5, 26/5, 29/5, 30/5, 31/5, 11/7, 8/8, 17/8
Payne, Rev., 12/7
pea meal, 15/6, 19/6
Pearse, Mrs., 18/3, 23/8, 1/9
Pechil (Pechell), Mr., 7/8

Pechil (Pechell), Mrs., 29/6, 7/8
pedal, 23/5, 24/11
petticoat, 3/5, 5/5, 13/5
Petty, Murray, 22/3, 24/3, 29/6
Phillips, Charley, 15/6, 18/6
photographs (photography, photos), 8/4, 5/5, 15/5, 26/5, 8/7, 23/7, 28/7, 1/8, 4/9
piano, 8/5
piano tuner, 4/5, 8/5
picnic, 2/5, 3/6, 7/6, 19/6, 21/6, 5/7, 26/7, 7/8, 21/8
Pink, Mr., 10/8
plaster, ginger, 3/5
Polly/Pollie, Aunt, 25/3, 15/4, 2/5 18/5, 5/8, 12/8
Pontifex, Mrs., 8/5
pony show, 26/4
pook, 22/6
Poor Old Joe, 1/4.
Pope, Mr and Mrs., 29/5, 1/6, 5/6
Poppet (pony), 23/5, 14/7, 19/7, 8/8
Portsmouth, 26/5
Post Office, 28/3, 5/4
postal order, 1/7
postman, 11/5
Poulner (Ringwood), 19/7
pram, 27/7
Puck Pits, 2/6
Pumpkin (dog), 1/5, 4/5, 10/5, 5/6, 11/6, 6/7, 7/7, 8/7, 26/7, 28/7, 29/7, 2/8, 4/8, 12/8, 16/8, 18/8, 19/8, 24/8
puncture, 17/5, 1/6, 29/6

Queens Road, 23/5

rabbit/s, 1/6, 5/6, 7/6, 21/6
rate collector, 30/5
Red Indian, 12/4
Reilly, Mr. James, 23/7
Rene, 22/5
Retford, Mr. William, 19/4
Retford, Mrs. Jane, 19/4, 3/6, 10/8
rheumatism, 18/3
Rhinefield, 21/6, 19/7
rhododendrons, 31/5
Ria, see Rye
rifle, 28/7, 29/7
Ringwood, 26/4, 11/5, 20/5, 13/6, 1/9, 9/9
Robert Bruce, 28/3
Robinson, Miss Sarah, 27/4, 3/6, 9/6
Romanist, 23/4
romps, 13/7
Rose/Rosie, 18/5, 21/5, 22/5, 25/5, 26/5
Rough (dog), 19/6, 4/9
Rufus Stone, 26/5, 7/8
Rush Moors, 12/7
Russell, Mr., 19/4
Russell, Mrs., 19/4
Ruthie (see Lambert, Ruthie)
Rye (Ria) (Maria Kelly), 14/3, 16/3, 15/4, 8/6, 13/6, 22/7, 12/8

saddle, bicycle, 20/5
saddle, horse, see side saddle
St. Luke, 23/4
St. Paul, 23/4
Salisbury, 22/4, 6/5, 10/5, 18/7
Sampson, Mr., 3/3, 4/3, 5/3, 12/3, 22/3, 25/3, 15/6, 19/6
Sanatorium, 17/5
Saul, Miss, 5/4
Saul, Mr., 5/4
Saul, Mrs., 5/4
saw bench, 10/7
Scamell, Rev. Tom Webb, 7/5, 17/6, 12/7
Scamell, Mrs., 10/7, 11/7, 25/7, 4/8
Scotland, 27/7
Scott Gally, 16/5
scythe, 12/6
separator (milk), 20/7
Seward, Mrs., 28/5, 29/5, 1/6, 2/6, 3/6, 4/6, 5/6
Seymour, C., 4/3, 15/6
Shaw, Mr., 14/3
shawls, 1/4
Sheldon, Charles Monroe, 28/3, 24/4
shoes, 28/3
shopping, 12/5
Short, Frederick Golden, 30/4, 9/6, 17/6, 30/6, 8/7, 23/7, 28/7, 29/7, 1/8, 5/8, 13/8, 20/8
Short, John Golden, 14/4, 7/6, 12/6, 17/6, 25/7, 5/8
Short, Miss, 8/3, 25/7
Shorts, 8/4, 23/5
side saddle, 4/5, 27/7
Sims, Mr., 10/3, 9/4
Singer (bicycle), 17/4, 11/5, 18/8
Slufters, 6/5
Smith, Mr and Mrs., 15/5
smoking, 25/7
snow, 20/3, 22/3, 23/3
Sociable (tricycle), 22/4
Sparebrook National, 10/3
sparrow, 18/7
Song without Words, 23/4
Southampton, 3/3, 7/3, 10/3, 17/3, 29/3, 7/4, 21/4, 6/5, 10/5, 18/5, 17/6, 23/6, 30/6, 7/7, 14/7, 17/7, 28/7, 11/8, 14/8, 7/9
Spirit of Christ, The, 19/4
Spring Song, 23/4
Squire (boys), 24/6
Squires, Mr., 5/3
Stag, Mr., 7/7
Stairs (Stares), Mr and Mrs., 4/8, 7/8
Stansbridge, Sophie, 20/8
Starling, Miss, 22/7, 24/7, 26/7, 28/7, 30/7, 31/7, 2/8
station (railway), 26/5, 27/5, 6/6, 10/6, 29/6, 6/7, 2/8, 23/8
Stephenson, 18/3
Stinking (H)edges, 9/8
stirrup, 7/5
Stoney Cross, 5/3, 14/3, 5/4, 15/5, 27/7
Stride, Joe, 16/8
Stride, Miss, 16/8

suit, 18/8
Sunday at H., 30/7
Sunday School, 4/6, 18/6, 23/7, 13/8
sunsets, 5/5
Surbiton, 11/4, 15/7
Swan Hill, 8/3, 2/5
Sydney (cousin), 30/3, 31/3, 1/4, 4/4, 6/4, 8/4, 9/4, 10/4, 13/5

Tame, Henry (junior), see Dada
Tame, Henry ('Old'), see Grandpa
Tame, Henry, see Harry (brother)
Tame, C. Mrs., 4/3
Tame, James (Uncle), 23/6, 30/6
Tame, Letitia, Mrs., see Mama
Tame, Mr. Richard, see Dick, Uncle
Tame, Richard, see Dick (brother)
Tame, Sydney, see Sydney (cousin)
Tame, William, see Will/Willie
Tammie's grave, 18/4, 20/4
tandem, 3/4.
Tanner, C., 31/7
Taylor, Arthur, 13/8
Taylor, Miss B., 25/4
Taylor, Laura, 1/7, 3/7, 4/7, 5/7, 6/7
Taylor, Mr., 31/3, 25/4, 10/5, 28/5, 1/6, 7/6
Taylor, Mrs., 4/3, 1/6, 23/6
tea fight, 12/7
telegram, 8/5, 9/5
telegraph boy, 4/7
Testwood, 3/6
Thorney Hill, 30/5, 7/8
thrush, 13/7, 18/7
thunder flies, 19/8
thunderstorm (thunder, thundery), 21/7, 22/7, 23/7, 19/8, 6/9, 7/9
tie-pins, 17.8
tonsils, 22/5
tooth (toothache, teeth), 17/3, 20/3, 21/3, 22/3, 3/5, 9/5, 15/5, 17/5, 17/7, 11/8
Topsy (pony), 10/5, 17/5
Totton, 30/5
train, 6/4, 22/4, 24/4, 8/5, 10/6, 17/7, 8/8, 14/8, 7/9
tramp, a, 3/4.
Tregold, Mr., 14/5
Trent, 27/5, 30/5, 6/6
Trusty Servant, 7/8
Tuck, Mr., 17/5
Tulip (cow), 27/7
Tunbridge Wells, 6/7, 20/7
turf, 2/6
turf spade, 5/5
Twentieth Door, The, 24/4
Twiggs Lane end Farm, 3/6

vases, 1/8, 16/8
Veeder Cyclometer, 13/5, 22/5, 8/7
Venn, Mr., 2/5
Venvell, Hubert, 6/3, 7/3, 30/4, 2/5, 20/5

Venvell, Mr., 3/3, 6/3, 7/3, 20/5, 22/5, 1/6, 14/6, 16/6, 23/6, 6/9
Venvell, Mrs., 28/3, 9/4, 14/4, 19/4, 8/5, 20/5, 22/5, 26/5, 31/5, 1/6, 14/6, 21/6, 23/6
Venvells, 8/4
vessel (Jack Kelly's), 10/3, 1/5
Vicarage, 4/6, 3/7

Ware, 21/7
Warr, Mr., 29/5
Watch stand, 23/5
Waterhouse, Mr., 8/3
Webb, Alice, 10/4
Webb, Arthur, 19/8, 21/8, 23/8, 24/8, 1/9, 6/9, 9/9
Webb, Maude (see Maude)
Wellman, Mr., 22/5
Wells, Mr., 4/5
Wesleyan, 23/4
West End (Southampton), 14/6
Westward Ho, 10/4
wheeler, 4, 23/5
White, 21/6
White, Dr Barrington, 22/6
Whitefoot (pony), 24/7, 23/8, 9/9
Whiteparish, 2/6, 18/7, 20/7
Wilkinson, Miss, 5/9
Will/Willie (brother), frequent references.
William, Uncle, 15/4, 29/5
Winchester, 11/7, 31/7
Winder, Miss, 25/3
Winsor, 1/5, 28/5, 1/6, 12/8, 24/8
wire, see telegram
Witt, Mr., 9/5
Woman of Samaria, The, 23/4
Woodford, 5/5, 2/6, 4/8, 7/8, 9/8
Worrall, Mrs., 7/6
Wright, Mr and Mrs., 10/7

Xmas, 10/4, 15/6

Young, Mr., 18/3, 22/3, 23/3